WHAT MADE ME LOVE ME: SIX STRATEGIES TO LIVE

F.I.E.R.C.E.

Kimberly Rashawn, MEd, BCPC

With Foreword by: Elder Michele Aikens
Closing Chapter Prayers by: Prophetess Tanya Wormely

WHAT MADE ME LOVE ME
Six Strategies to Live F.I. E.R.C.E.

Copyright © 2018 by Kimberly Rashawn, M.Ed., BCPC

With Foreword by: Elder Michele Aikens

Closing Chapter Prayers by: Prophetess Tanya Wormely

All rights reserved. No part of this publication may be reproduced or transmitted in any form or by any means, including informational storage and retrieval systems, without permission in writing from the copyright holder, except for brief quotations in a review and certain other noncommercial uses permitted by copyright law.

ISBN: 978-1-7322384-6-6

Interior Design by AugustPride, LLC

Book cover and Logo Design credit: Digital Art and Design by Veronica Nicole

ILLUMINATION PRESS
1100 Peachtree Street, Suite 250
Atlanta, Georgia 30309
United States

Table of Contents

Acknowledgement (This is for You, Abba) 01
Thank You (I appreciate you) 03
Dedications (Forever in my heart) 07
Shout Outs 09
Disclaimer 11
Foreword 13
Preface (A letter to my readers) 15
Introduction (The Launch of a Movement) 21
How to Use This Book 39
Who Do I Turn To? 43
Fearless 47
Innovative 75
Empowered 89
Resilient 103
Confident 123
Exuberant 145
What Made Me Love Me: Analyzing the Process 179
Time for Restoration and Renewal 209
Call to Salvation 213
F.I.E.R.C.E. Women's Empowerment Movement 215
About the Author 219
Complete List of Affirmations 223

"So now faith, hope, and love abide, these three; but the greatest of these is love."

1 Corinthians 13:13, English Standard Version

ACKNOWLEDGEMENT

This is for You, Abba

To The One Who Saved My Life:
Only God would take my pain and make it painless.
Only God would take my test and make it a testimony.
Only God would stretch me in order for me to reach my full potential
Thank You, Lord, for all You have done for me!

Abba,
I cannot believe this is actually happening.
I am in awe of the doors You opened for me to tell this story of transformation.
Thank You for everything: the good, the bad, the ugly, and the better.
All of it made me who I am today.

All that I am and all that I am destined to be is because of You
When I gave up on me, You held me close and allowed me time to heal
You understand my flaws and my faults
And yet, You still love me
You saved me from gunfire, my abusers, and myself
You are my Secret Place and my Sustainer
Your love is irreplaceable, indescribable, and unconditional
Thank You for being my Source
Without You, I am nothing
Thank you for accepting me and embracing me
You are so awesome!

Humbly and lovingly submitted,
Kimberly Rashawn

THANK YOU
I appreciate you

To my Mom: Thank you for instilling the importance of being able to hold an intelligent conversation with others and giving me the foundation of education and knowledge. I appreciate all you have done for me. I love you, Mummie!

❤❤❤❤❤❤❤❤

To my Daughter: Your birth gave my life new meaning. You mean so much to me! I thank God for you, and for the gift you are to me and to so many others. Mommi loves you, and through the grace of God, I will continually fulfill the promise I made to you while you were in my womb. Thank you for your support, love, belief in me, and for being my biggest cheerleader by standing by me and pushing me to achieve my goals and walk in my purpose. God gave me a perfect example of love when He blessed me to be your mother. #LoveIsInIt

❤❤❤❤❤❤❤❤

To Bril: You are forever a part of me. You inspire me in so many ways. I am so proud of the man you have become. Thank you for always being there at the right moment. I am so glad we are reconnected. You are a part of the missing link of my life. Love you always! #Fam4Ever

To Terrell: Blessings come in various forms. You are such a blessing to me. You blessed me with the gift of love and helped me realize it was okay to trust, care, and love again. Thank you for showing me what real love looks and feels like, and for giving me so many reasons to smile. I love you, honeyy! #OurLove

❤❤❤❤❤❤❤❤

To The Whitmans: Thank you for embracing and taking me and my daughter into your family. I truly appreciate your support and love. You will always hold a very special place in my heart.

❤❤❤❤❤❤❤❤

To Wally: Thank you for always encouraging me and looking out for me and my daughter. Thank you for speaking into my life when you said I had a tiger's pounce. You are a true blessing to my life and I will always be there for you. You are the best godfather ever.

❤❤❤❤❤❤❤❤

To Lisa F: You have been a true blessing to me and baby girl over the years. I thank God for you daily. Thanks for our many talks and allowing me to breathe. I appreciate you more than you will ever know.

To my Cousins: I am so glad we are reconnected. We are stronger together than wer are apart. Always remember we have strong genes that make us unique, creative, and fantabulous. # famILY

❤❤❤❤❤❤❤❤

To Athena M, Jeanine B, Kina A, Sharming N, and Trinette W: Thank you for your sisterhood and friendship. You loved on me during some very difficult times in my life and continue to stand by me no matter what. I am grateful and appreciative of our connection.

❤❤❤❤❤❤❤

To my god children: You are a part of the reason that I strive and grind so hard. No matter what … always stay focused and never give up.

❤❤❤❤❤❤❤❤

To Franklin: Thank you for pushing me out of the nest even when I did not want to fly. Thank you for your patience as I wrestled with the attack I was under. Thank you for always speaking into my purpose and my destiny. You are a great Spiritual brother.

To Tanya Wormely: Thank you for writing the prayers for the end of each chapter. They provided the spark that was needed to complete other prayers and sections of the book. Your servant heart is greatly appreciated. May God continue to enrich every area of your life.

♥♥♥♥♥♥♥♥

To Michele Aikens: I have gleaned from you from afar for many years. You are a true inspiration to so many people, including me. Thank you for blessing this book by writing the foreword. I am excited about our new connection.

♥♥♥♥♥♥♥♥

To Benecia Ponder: Your belief in me helped me birth this book. Thank you for listening to me ramble at times in order to help birth the vision and for being an awesome mentor. I thank God for our divine connection and love how you were able to pull so much out of me.

DEDICATIONS
Forever In My Heart

This book is dedicated to you because you are so special to me and in some way you were a reason I developed a love for myself and walked in my purpose. I am very appreciative of all you did for me during our time together. I will always carry each of you in my heart. I thank God for the time we spent together.

Uncle, **Carl**

Maternal great-grandmother, **Granny Ruth**

Maternal grandmother, **Granny**

Spiritual sister, **Gina**

Spiritual mom, **Prophetess Frances**

Godmother, **Deborah Denise**

Thank you for your love and support over the years. You played awesome roles in my life and I thank you for the impact you made on my life. I miss you so much!

My daddy, *Gypsy*

You always pushed me to achieve more, but I never knew how. Losing you was my hardest life test. I wanted you to be here physically when I finally completed this book, but I will carry on your legacy. Thank you for instilling values, morals, and standards in me via our many talks (that I called lectures LOL). I would give my last to be able to hear your voice, laugh with you, watch Matlock and the Golden Girls together, and smell the aroma of orange Certs coming from you. I hope I am making you proud. I miss you so much, daddy! #DaddysGirl

❤❤❤❤❤❤❤

"I thank my God upon every remembrance of you"

• Philippians 1:3, King James Version•

Shout Outs

To Monique Caradine and Sylvia Duncan: Who knew one phone call would be just what was needed to provide me with the necessary tools to soar? God knew! Thank you so much for the words you spoke into me. Together, we are #ClimbingHigher!

To J. J. Smith: Thank you for the 10-Day Green Smoothie Cleanse because it helped me gain control of my eating. When my book arrived, I read it all the time to gain a full understanding of the cleanse. This cleanse helped me receive amazing results and I felt great afterwards. #GSC #GS4L

To Ladonna F: Thank you for your amazing fitness transformation program which provided the necessary jumpstart I needed to go after my goals. #iChooseFitness

To Veronica Nicole: Thank you so much for your support and designing several projects for of this book and the women's movement. I am so glad to have found an awesome graphics artist/branding specialist to be a part of this awesome movement and what is to come. I value your artistic gift and cherish our new friendship. #TheBestIsYetToCome

Disclaimer

This is a story about my life. It discloses some of the things that held me back, kept me bound, and made me view myself as less than. In no way is any of the information disclosed to judge, hurt, or discredit anyone. This book was written from a place of peace in efforts to help other people struggling with abuse, rejection, hurt, mistrust, abandonment, neglect, and feeling unloved. This book was written to empower people by informing them that they do not have to continue to live life in a hurtful state of mind and provides strategies to change the status quo of their life by changing their perspective of life and renewing their mind.

Once I came to grips with the root of what I was experiencing, I began to live life differently; whereas I gained control instead of allowing my past and my emotions to control me. This book outlines my journey of how I became F.I.E.R.C.E., and how you can apply the six strategies to become F.I.E.R.C.E. as well.

This book does not guarantee to have the answers to life's challenges and only serves as a template and guide to live a F.I.E.R.C.E. lifestyle.

Foreword

We women manage a lot – nicely. Depending on your age, you were socialized to not get your dress dirty, play nicely with others, don't talk too much about yourself and DON'T BE A THREAT TO ANYONE. While those things are ...nice at eight or nine, they don't serve you well when it is time to break out of the boxes of others' imposing.

Sometimes you're going to have to get dirty. I don't mean playing dirty or cheating others. I mean you may have to get dirty from trying and falling; your emotional knees get skinned and the armor you perfected to keep you safe gets ripped. Those times when you are no longer pretending to be ok may look like a dirty, tear-stained face as you sit with your questions and coffee before the rest of the house wakes up.

Playing nicely with others isn't always possible either as you reach for your goals. Of course, we are to love others as God loves us, but that doesn't mean relationships won't suffer. Breaking out of a box means some others will be uncomfortable. *If you come out of the box, who will help us maintain our mediocrity?* Playing nice means not always going along with others' expectations, but answering the call to Divine PURPOSE.

Oh, and not talking too much about yourself… at some point you are going to have to declare who you are and WHY you

are for those who don't believe. This is not to say that you will become prideful, but you must own the gifts, callings, and purpose God has called you to, and somebody must know it.

Now I smile as I think about how not to be a threat to anyone. It is a lifelong game of talking too softly, speaking without impact, and walking only where there are crowds. As you step into all of who you are called to be, you *__will__* threaten somethings: You will pose a threat to ignorance as you teach others how to walk boldly. You will become a threat to mediocrity when you begin to operate in excellence. You will threaten every aimless individual in your life when you start to walk in purpose. To live boldly is to threaten everything created by fear.

When I see words like "Fierce", I think of a tiger or female lion who is ready to tear anything apart that stands between it and its prey. If your prey is purpose, how willing are you to eliminate what stands between you and it?

Be FIERCE in your pursuit of the YOU God created. You won't get to it any other way.

Elder Michele Aikens

PREFACE
A Letter to my Readers

"Though she be but little, she is fierce."

• **William Shakespeare** •

I am so glad you are reading this page. Please continue to read not only this page, but the entire book. I wrote this book as a tool to empower women. This book embarks not only on the journey of my life of what made me love me, but provides insight of how I discovered my purpose, learned the importance self-empowerment, and why I began to live a F.I.E.R.C.E. lifestyle.

See, I know what it feels like to experience self-hatred and to never think you are good enough. I know what it feels like to seek love in all the wrong places, as well as constantly searching for a missing piece of your identity that no one seems to have. Unfortunately, I was a victim of several abusive relationships before the age of 25, which left me feeling isolated and afraid. As a teenager, I was a self-labeled manic depressant and used to hide in my closet wondering if anyone knew I was not around or cared enough to find me. I attempted suicide when I was in my early twenties.

Even while serving in ministry, I was shunned and exiled. All of this drove me closer to God and further away from people. At most points in my life, I felt like there was no one I could trust due to the numerous people who had abused me, turned their

back on me, and/or neglected me. For almost four years, I hid my face and gave a smile when needed to; all along attempting to fake it until I made it, but internally I was a mess.

As a way of shielding myself from the pains of life, I encased myself in a self-made bubble so no one could hurt me again. I even built a wall around my heart to secure it from being broken again. I felt secure within my bubble and behind my wall. I did not care if I lived or died because my only reason for living was to raise my daughter. During that time, I was not living; but instead, I merely existed and did what I needed to do to survive. That is until the day God spoke a word to me that empowered me and changed my life.

F.I.E.R.C.E. was the word God spoke to me, which is an acronym for:

Fearless • Innovative • Empowered • Resilient • Confident • Exuberant

Over the years, God had been taking me on a journey of overcoming my past and my fears. This journey became the mechanism that birthed living a F.I.E.R.C.E. lifestyle. Now, I want to empower and equip you to live a F.I.E.R.C.E. lifestyle as well.

I will admit sometimes it is hard to live a happy, go lucky lifestyle. You feel as though your life is a façade of happiness. I get it. Been there; done that. Understand this…we are entitled to a day in which things are not as great as they should be. Hey, it is life and stuff happens. The thing I want to stress is do not to allow yourself to stay there.

I say this because I allowed myself to stay in my bubble for too long and it was actually doing me more harm than good. When Moses died, God told Joshua it was time to get into position for what was next (read Joshua 1). Yes, with all that is going on in your life it can be hard to smile in the midst of your pain, but God is calling you to shake yourself loose and trust His process along the road to recovery and self-empowerment.

Reason for Writing this Book
You are the reason I wrote this book. The purpose of this book is to help women overcome the obstacles in their life that are enabling them, and equip them with strategies to not only love themselves, but also live a F.I.E.R.C.E. lifestyle of self-empowerment and self-worth.

The process will not happen overnight and reliving your past will be painful, but it is important that you are truthful with yourself by acknowledging what is deterring you and go through each strategy of this process. No longer will you keep things on the back burner, but actually deal with what you are going through. The six strategies and daily affirmations are designed to empower you and renew your mind.

In the life application sections, you are able to journal what you will do to break through the glass ceiling that is keeping you from being free. According to Google Dictionary, a glass ceiling is "an unofficially acknowledged barrier to advancement

in a profession, especially affecting women and members of minorities." The time has come to break through the glass ceilings that others have created over you as well as the ones you created over yourself in order to be totally free, empowered, and walk in your purpose.

The best way to walk in self-empowerment is to be honest when it comes to journaling and answering the questions throughout this book. This book will take you on a personal journey of your life – past, present, and future. There are no right or wrong answers; this is your life story that needs mending and healing. These are not six things telling you what to do to become self-empowered. This book is packed with six strategies that will lead you to living an empowered lifestyle. According to Google Dictionary, strategy is defined as "a plan of action or policy designed to achieve a major or overall aim." The process will be life changing if you are honest as you go through each strategy of the journey. One of the best pieces of advice my mother gave me was, "In order to be truthful with others, first you have to be truthful and honest with yourself." How bad do you want your freedom? You deserve it and God wants you to be free.

> *"So if the Son sets you free, you will be free indeed"*
> • **John 8:36, New International Version** •

It is time for you to be free! To what extent will you go through to obtain your freedom? The answer lies within you. No one can want for you what you do not want for yourself. Freedom, from

our past and the things holding us back, is a choice each of us has to make for our self.

From this book, you will learn how to empower yourself because when no one is around or answering their phone, I need you to be able to speak life back into yourself and believe that you are an overcomer. You will learn the process of renewing your mind so you can rid yourself of stinking thinking (negative words or thoughts). Negative thoughts and negative words are not allowed. You will have daily affirmations to speak life to dead and desolate areas of your mind and soul to empower yourself. There is so much in store as we take this journey together. Are you ready? I know it might seem scary, but know this … I am with you every step of the way. I have been on this journey and I thank God for processing me to be F.I.E.R.C.E. Becoming F.I.E.R.C.E. saved my life. #Let'sDoThis

Even while writing this book, I was hit from various angles. Living a F.I.E.R.C.E. lifestyle was tried and tested. Several questions were at stake as I endured these tests. Do I revert and go back to life within my self-made bubble and behind my wall? Or do I stand fearless and resilient because I am an overcomer? When I tell you having a renewed mind is important, it really is. Not only was I tested, but I was able to bounce back from each hit. Your girl bobbed, weaved, threw some upper cuts, and came out victorious. Do I guarantee to have all of the answers? Of course I do not have all of the answers, I am not God, but I can

tell you God is awesome and He wants the best for His people. I can tell you being empowered and having a renewed mind helps when life's obstacles occur. When you are equipped to encourage yourself, you are able to work through any situation.

Remember when David had to encourage himself?

> *"And David was greatly distressed; for the people spake of stoning him, because the soul of all the people was grieved, every man for his sons and for his daughters: but David encouraged himself in the Lord his God*
>
> • 1 Samuel 30:6, King James Version •

I can say this…you will learn to encourage yourself in the Lord; that is what self-empowerment is all about.

Now, let's embark on this journey of developing self-empowerment and self-love so we can live a F.I.E.R.C.E. lifestyle.

Humbly submitted,

Kimberly Rashawn

> *"I am not who other people desired or wanted me to be, instead I became who I was purposed and destined to be."*
>
> • **Kimberly Rashawn** •

INTRODUCTION
The Launch of a Movement

Proverbs 31 Woman

When I think of a F.I.E.R.C.E. woman, I instantly think of the Proverbs 31 Woman. Let's learn more about the Proverbs 31 Woman, how she is F.I.E.R.C.E., and how she relates to today's woman.

Proverbs 31:10-31, King James Version

> [10] Who can find a virtuous woman? for her price is far above rubies.
> [11] The heart of her husband doth safely trust in her, so that he shall have no need of spoil.
> [12] She will do him good and not evil all the days of her life.
> [13] She seeketh wool, and flax, and worketh willingly with her hands.
> [14] She is like the merchants' ships; she bringeth her food from afar.
> [15] She riseth also while it is yet night, and giveth meat to her household, and a portion to her maidens.
> [16] She considereth a field, and buyeth it: with the fruit of her hands she planteth a vineyard.
> [17] She girdeth her loins with strength, and strengtheneth her arms.
> [18] She perceiveth that her merchandise is good: her candle goeth not out by night.

[19] She layeth her hands to the spindle, and her hands hold the distaff.
[20] She stretcheth out her hand to the poor; yea, she reacheth forth her hands to the needy.
[21] She is not afraid of the snow for her household: for all her household are clothed with scarlet.
[22] She maketh herself coverings of tapestry; her clothing is silk and purple.
[23] Her husband is known in the gates, when he sitteth among the elders of the land.
[24] She maketh fine linen, and selleth it; and delivereth girdles unto the merchant.
[25] Strength and honour are her clothing; and she shall rejoice in time to come.
[26] She openeth her mouth with wisdom; and in her tongue is the law of kindness.
[27] She looketh well to the ways of her household, and eateth not the bread of idleness.
[28] Her children arise up, and call her blessed; her husband also, and he praiseth her.
[29] Many daughters have done virtuously, but thou excellest them all.
[30] Favour is deceitful, and beauty is vain: but a woman that feareth the Lord, she shall be praised.
[31] Give her of the fruit of her hands; and let her own works praise her in the gates.

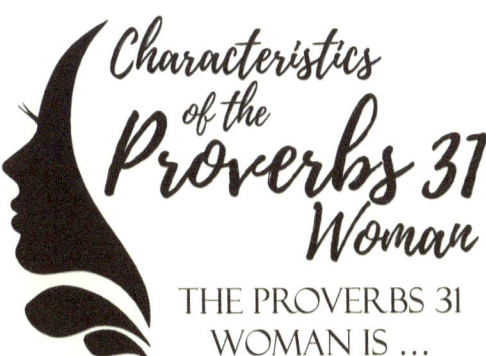

Characteristics of the Proverbs 31 Woman

THE PROVERBS 31 WOMAN IS ...

Valuable
VERSE 10

Trust Worthy
VERSES 11-12

Resourceful
VERSES 13-14

Generous
VERSE 15

Adored
VERSE 31

God Fearing
VERSE 30

Virtuous
VERSE 29

Blessed
VERSE 28

Wise
VERSES 25-27

Respected
VERSES 23-24

Entrepreneur
VERSES 16-17

Kind
VERSE 20

Prepareds
VERSES 18-19

Creative
VERSES 21-22

F.I.E.R.C.E.
infographic

The Proverbs 31 Woman…

- knows how to make ends meet and she knows how to take care of her family.

- knows her role in the household, marketplace, and life.

- is submissive. She knows when to speak and when to keep silent. Her silence speaks volumes.

- has lived a life that has sent obstacles which caused her to exhibit her resiliency, and during the time of enduring the obstacles, there was always praise on her lips.

- is creative due to her ability to make tapestries and clothing.

- is admired due to her stature in the family, and everyone looks to her for answers and assistance.

- is an atmosphere changer. When she walks into a room, all eyes are on her because she is confident and radiant. There is an aura about her whereas people automatically gravitate to her.

Who is the Proverbs 31 Woman?

The Proverbs 31 Woman is you! Have you ever pictured or considered yourself to be like the Proverbs 31 Woman? If not, what is holding you back from being all you can be? Who is

stopping you from walking in your purpose and fulfilling your destiny? Is it your friends? Are family members deterring you? Or perhaps, you might be the one standing in the way of becoming all you were purposed and destined to become?

After reading this book and applying the life application activities, you will see yourself in a new light. You will understand your life is valuable and you will be equipped with tools to walk in your purpose; just like the Proverbs 31 Woman.

Before you can see the value in others, you must understand your own worth and know you are valuable. You are a precious commodity. Remember verse 10 said, "Her price is far above rubies." The time has come to break away from negative thinking. The time has come to be free, shine, and walk in your purpose and in full freedom (from your past and all forms of negativity).

How does the Proverbs 31 Woman connect to today's woman?

Today's woman is resourceful, and for various reasons, she knows how to make ends meet. Unfortunately, in some circumstances, today's woman is the head of the household, and for this reason, she has to provide for her family alone. Rest assured that even though the book of Proverbs was written thousands of years ago, the Proverbs 31 Woman is still relevant today. With the different things happening in society, it is time to empower young girls, youth, and women to liken themselves to

the Proverbs 31 Woman because she is a fearless, innovative, empowered, resilient, confident, exuberant human being. All of my F.I.E.R.C.E. Proverbs 31 Women make some noise!!!!!!!!!

F.I.E.R.C.E.

According to Google Dictionary, fierce is defined as "(of a feeling, emotion, or action) showing a heartfelt and powerful intensity."

F.I.E.R.C.E Women's Empowerment Movement will launch Fall 2018, and serves as a mechanism to empower women around the world. This book is a tool to help women lead a F.I.E.R.C.E. lifestyle of self-empowerment and self-love.

F.I.E.R.C.E. is an acronym for:

Fearless • Innovative • Empowered • Resilient • Confident • Exuberant

It is so easy to be empowered by other people. Unfortunately, these are often temporary, get right quick fixes that last a few hours or days because other baggage from life inhibits the information that was received to effectively exhibit change. Our goal is to provide tools that will lead to permanent empowerment so the lessons and tools learned at workshops and seminars will stick. Only then can real change occur.

Each strategy is contingent upon each other in order to detangle the snares of the enemy that have held you bound and release the power that has been lying dormant within you. For this

reason, it is very important to go in order and not skip any of the strategies, pages, or sections.

Why living a F.I.E.R.C.E. lifestyle is important?

Living a F.I.E.R.C.E. lifestyle is important because it leads to self-empowerment and self-love. The six strategies of living a F.I.E.R.C.E. lifestyle set the tone for renewing your mind and breaking the glass ceiling of confinement that we have created for ourselves as well as detach the strongholds that are entangling us. I must admit this is a hands-on, dig deep, have some tissue next to you type of experience. We are going to dig into the hidden areas that have been covered by layers of Band-Aids. We will remove the mask that has been worn so people do not see the pain of your true identity. We will get to the core and root of your pain, expose it, and denounce and cut off the root. We will uncover why you feel the way you feel and provide strategies that will not cover your wounds, but instead heal and restore broken areas of your life.

You ask, "Why is living a F.I.E.R.C.E. lifestyle important?" Living a F.I.E.R.C.E. lifestyle is important because you owe it to yourself to be free from the shackles of your past and empowered to live your best life.

F.I.E.R.C.E. equals becoming purpose driven and being prepared

There are two things you need to do to begin to live a F.I.E.R.C.E. lifestyle: (1) get clear on your purpose and (2) get prepared. Understanding your purpose is very important, and unfortunately, I find many people do not know what their purpose is. We were created to worship God. We can worship in our giving, worship in adoration of God, and worship by making disciples of men. For the sake of this book, we will concentrate on the latter. Jesus commanded us to make disciples of men, which simply means to go out and draw others into the Kingdom of God (read Matthew 28:19-20). Walking in your purpose helps draw others into the Kingdom of God.

Also, we need to get prepared because we never know when a great opportunity will present itself. Benjamin Franklin once said, "If you fail to plan, you are planning to fail." Planning is a vital component of the preparation process. Some people have a 'live life as it occurs' mentality, which is fine, but there will be a time when you will have to actually execute a plan in order to be effective and prepared. Going with the flow will only suffice for so long.

Get clear on your purpose

So often, I hear people say they do not know or understand what their purpose is. According to Google Dictionary, purpose is defined as "the reason for which something is done or created or for which something exists." You were created for purpose and with purpose. The essence of who you are serves a purpose. We

will help you discover your purpose in a later chapter.

We were born with gifts and talents to utilize. Oftentimes, we do not understand what drives our passion is what we were purposed to do. Know this… we have been called to be glory carriers for God. It is important that we understand and realize God created us with a purpose in mind.

> [28] And we know that all things work together for good to them that love God, to them who are the called according to his purpose.
> [29] For whom he did foreknow, he also did predestinate to be conformed to the image of his Son, that he might be the firstborn among many brethren.
> [30] Moreover whom he did predestinate, them he also called: and whom he called, them he also justified: and whom he justified, them he also glorified
>
> • **Romans 8:28-30, King James Version** •

The time has come for us to understand God predestined our lives while we were in our mother's womb. Yes, we might have taken detours from God's original plan, but God uses our tests and trials as a way to show His Sovereignty in our lives. Adam and Eve disobeyed God's commandment, and before He banished them from the Garden of Eden, He clothed them. Even after their fall, God still used them and prepared them for the next phase of their purpose (read Genesis 3:21).

How we hone and master our craft means a lot to God.

Consider the story of the parable of the talents found in Matthew 25:15-29, King James Version.

¹⁵ And unto one he gave five talents, to another two, and to another one; to every man according to his several ability; and straightway took his journey.

¹⁶ Then he that had received the five talents went and traded with the same, and made them other five talents.

¹⁷ And likewise he that had received two, he also gained other two.

¹⁸ But he that had received one went and digged in the earth, and hid his lord's money.

¹⁹ After a long time the lord of those servants cometh, and reckoneth with them.

²⁰ And so he that had received five talents came and brought other five talents, saying, Lord, thou deliveredst unto me five talents: behold, I have gained beside them five talents more.

²¹ His lord said unto him, Well done, thou good and faithful servant: thou hast been faithful over a few things, I will make thee ruler over many things: enter thou into the joy of thy lord.

²² He also that had received two talents came and said, Lord, thou deliveredst unto me two talents: behold, I have gained two other talents beside them.

²³ His lord said unto him, Well done, good and faithful servant; thou hast been faithful over a few things, I will make thee ruler over many things: enter thou into the joy of thy lord.

²⁴ Then he which had received the one talent came and said, Lord, I knew thee that thou art an hard man, reaping where thou hast not sown, and gathering where thou hast

not strawed:

²⁵ And I was afraid, and went and hid thy talent in the earth: lo, there thou hast that is thine.

²⁶ His lord answered and said unto him, Thou wicked and slothful servant, thou knewest that I reap where I sowed not, and gather where I have not strawed:

²⁷ Thou oughtest therefore to have put my money to the exchangers, and then at my coming I should have received mine own with usury.

²⁸ Take therefore the talent from him, and give it unto him which hath ten talents.

²⁹ For unto every one that hath shall be given, and he shall have abundance: but from him that hath not shall be taken away even that which he hath.

The ones who took their talents and worked them received a blessing from the Lord. Play close attention to what happened to the one who hid his talent – the Lord took it from him and gave it to the one with ten talents. When the Lord gives us a talent, it is important that we exercise, utilize, and grow what the Lord has given to us. How do you feel when you give someone a gift that they never use?

When we work what God has given to us, we cultivate our talents whereas it brings forth a harvest. We are able to double what God has blessed us with. This also draws others to want to know the God we serve. When we bury or hide our talents, they are not used to honor or glorify God in a manner that brings forth a harvest. How can others learn about God if we are not

activating what He placed inside of us so others can see His works in us? "Let your light so shine before men, that they may see your good works, and glorify your Father which is in heaven" (Matthew 5:16). Is your light shining brightly for all to see or is it a flashlight that you only use for you to navigate through life?

Get prepared

It is important that we are prepared at all times because we never know when we will be called to be used by God. Think of the parable of the 10 virgins found in Matthew 25-1-14.

> [1] Then shall the kingdom of heaven be likened unto ten virgins, which took their lamps, and went forth to meet the bridegroom.
> [2] And five of them were wise, and five were foolish.
> [3] They that were foolish took their lamps, and took no oil with them:
> [4] But the wise took oil in their vessels with their lamps.
> [5] While the bridegroom tarried, they all slumbered and slept.
> [6] And at midnight there was a cry made, Behold, the bridegroom cometh; go ye out to meet him.
> [7] Then all those virgins arose, and trimmed their lamps.
> [8] And the foolish said unto the wise, Give us of your oil; for our lamps are gone out.
> [9] But the wise answered, saying, Not so; lest there be not enough for us and you: but go ye rather to them that sell, and buy for yourselves.
> [10] And while they went to buy, the bridegroom came; and they

that were ready went in with him to the marriage: and the door was shut.

[11] Afterward came also the other virgins, saying, Lord, Lord, open to us.

[12] But he answered and said, Verily I say unto you, I know you not.

[13] Watch therefore, for ye know neither the day nor the hour wherein the Son of man cometh.

[14] For the kingdom of heaven is as a man travelling into a far country, who called his own servants, and delivered unto them his goods.

Check this out. There were ten virgins, but then the Bible characterizes them based on their level of preparation. Five of the ladies were wise and five of the ladies were foolish. The five foolish ladies did not take oil with them for their lamps, but the five wise ladies took their lamps and oil. By the time the bridegroom came, all of their lamps hand gone out, and the foolish ladies told the wise ladies to give them some of their oil. The wise ladies told the foolish ladies to go buy some oil because there was not enough to share. While they were gone to purchase more oil, the foolish ladies missed out on their opportunity to meet the bridegroom because they were not prepared.

Wow, are you kidding me?! You do not come prepared and then you want to take what I have to make up for your lack of preparation. It is real bold and inconsiderate to inconvenience someone else and want to take what they have because of your lack of preparation. For this reason, I raised my daughter

to be prepared by having a plan. Whenever she wanted to do something, she had to present a plan. Not only did this teach my daughter organizational skills, but it also taught her analytical and problem solving skills. Certain aspects of the plan might change, but at least there was a plan in place to go off. Adjustments can be made along the way, but when you do not have a plan, you are jacked up and can miss out on great opportunities in life.

How often have we gone through life aimlessly and unprepared, and as a result, missed out on awesome opportunities? No one knows when the bridegroom will return or when a great opportunity will present itself so it is important that we prepare ourselves accordingly. God has given each of us talents to be used for His glory. Instead of aimlessly walking through life without a plan, let's start planning accordingly. Once you begin to become more organized, you will realize you are not as stressed about things.

Being prepared might consist of having your business cards printed and with you at all times. It might consist of having a small notepad and pen near you at all times to write down your ideas or take notes. Another aspect of preparation might be to purchase a calendar or utilize the calendar in your cellular phone so you do not miss events or appointments. If you are seeking employment, putting your business suit in the cleaners so you are ready when you are called for a job interview would

be a means of preparation. There are so many ways to become more prepared. Take some time to think about it and begin to implement different strategies of preparation into your life so you do not miss out on great opportunities.

How becoming F.I.E.R.C.E. helped me break strongholds and become self-empowered

One day a friend called me and spoke into my life. Tears rolled down my face as she acknowledged the woman I had become and how she was so proud of me. These were some of her words… "Shawn, I am so happy for you. I just had to take the time to actually call you and let you know that. I did not want to send it through text message. This new person you have become – I like her. Don't ever go back to the way you were, but keep moving forward into all God has destined for you. If you go back, let it only be for a testimony, but keep up with what you are doing. I love this new you!"

Her words spoke volumes to my soul and empowered me. See, she knew I had been withdrawn and in a bubble. I left social media and only contacted people via text message to check on them or send people words of encouragement. During my time of being hidden, she would check on me and tell me something was not the same with me. I would say, "I am fine. I have been very busy with school." Guess what?! She did not believe my false sense of happiness. Her response would be, "Okay,

Shawn," along with thinking emojis. I did not go around people a lot during that season, especially if I knew they were capable of detecting my pain.

When I finally demolished the wall and burst my self-made bubble, I came out full force. I joined a fitness program and began to pour into me. God had been working on me and processing me for years. The time had finally come to be free from what was entangling and hurting me, and decide to let go of the pain and hurt that was weighing me down. Let me say that again… decide to let go of the pain. Remember, I said freedom from our past was a choice? Sometimes the decision is ours to let go of what is entangling us. It was time for me to live and execute a F.I.E.R.C.E. lifestyle. I knew it was in me, I just did not want to be hurt, called strange, feel unwanted, or experience rejection again.

As I was preparing to write this book, I came across a prophetic word the Lord spoke to me and I was in tears of how He told me years ago of the process He was going to take me through (it is shared in a later chapter). There were times I reverted and decided to stay in my cocoon longer, but when I finally broke through, it was on and popping. Let me share this disclaimer … life happens and life is filled with ups and downs. Even as I was finishing this book I experienced pain and had to take time to encourage myself. I want you to know when life has you feeling as though you are on the down side of the see saw that you have to options – break free and get off or push hard so that you can

make it so you are up again. Those options come with a renewed mind, which we will discuss in later chapter.

Time to break through your own glass ceiling and strongholds

The time has come for you to break through the glass ceiling and strongholds that are inhibiting you from walking in your purpose and being empowered to overcome life's obstacles. So many things occur in our life that will make us feel defeated, rejected, unappreciated, and unloved. Those feelings can have a lasting effect on us and tend to confine us in our own world that is isolated from others. Well, the time has come for that mentality to change. The time has come to break through the glass ceiling that you keep hitting when you try to excel. The time has come to tear down the strongholds that have entangled you. The time has come to break forth! The time has come to be free!

⁴ (For the weapons of our warfare are not carnal, but mighty through God to the pulling down of strong holds;) 5 Casting down imaginations, and every high thing that exalteth itself against the knowledge of God, and bringing into captivity every thought to the obedience of Christ

• **2 Corinthians 10:4-5, King James Version** •

Are you ready to live a F.I.E.R.C.E. lifestyle?

Are you tired of doing the same thing and getting the same or worst results? Are you ready to make a change in your life? Well, you are in the right place at the right time. Life is full of

tests and trials, and it is how we handle those tests and trails that either sustain us or break us. It is time to rid ourselves of our old mentalities and methodologies by renewing our mind.

How are you using what God has given you? Are you growing your talents or hiding them? Are you making necessary changes to be prepared for what is to come? Do you have a plan? "And the Lord answered me, and said, Write the vision, and make it plain upon tables, that he may run that readeth it" (Habakkuk 2:2). This book will serve as a catalyst for you to write the vision, utilize your talents, and understand your purpose.

This book is not to speak to the woman you want to be. We are speaking to the woman you were destined and designed to be. You are an original. There is no one else like you. No copycats or knock-offs allowed. It is time for you to soar, break free, and shine bright like a diamond. It is time to be F.I.E.R.C.E.

I am extremely elated that you are ready and willing to take this journey of discovering self-empowerment and self-love. I am eager and ready to help you realize your potential. Empowering others and seeing people set free really excites me! I am so excited about your future! Now, let's embark on this journey together along the path that leads to self-empowerment and living a F.I.E.R.C.E. lifestyle. #Let'sGetIt

How to Use this Book

Thank you for purchasing my book. I am excited that you are interested in learning the six strategies to live a F.I.E.R.C.E. lifestyle.

Please note: This book is not just a reading experience, but instead, this is a journey of developing self-empowerment and self-love which leads to living a F.I.E.R.C.E. lifestyle.

If you did not read the Foreword, Preface, and Introduction, please read them now. These sections have powerful information and insight as to how to navigate through this book, what to expect from this journey, and provide empowering messages about self-empowerment. These sections set the course and tone for the book and other chapters make referencing points of information found in these sections; so please read them. Go page by page. You will not regret it.

Daily Affirmations

Near the end of each chapter, you will have daily affirmations to recite. Do not skip this process. The daily affirmations might seem redundant, but there is a reason for the redundancy. See, for years you heard things such as 'you are a failure' or 'you won't succeed', and your brain programmed itself to believe such nonsense. Well, now the time has come to reprogram your brain to hear something new and positive. We want the affirmations to resonate in your Spirit.

Reflection Moments

Each strategy has reflection moments after reciting the daily affirmations and life applications exercises to help you break through areas that are hindering you. As a mentor and personal development coach, I like to incorporate journaling and reflection as a way of overcoming obstacles and moving forward. Once you have finished reflecting and journaling, there are prayers to affirm and strengthen you after each strategy.

Life Stories

The life stories are parts of my life that helped me walk in the six strategies. These six strategies are what made me love me and become self-empowered. These strategies lead to living a F.I.E.R.C.E. lifestyle. Living a F.I.E.R.C.E. lifestyle is not arrogance or cockiness. It is the ability to overcome life's situations, lean on and trust God, be confident in who God called you to be, and develop self-love. So many life experiences have made us question who we are or where we are going, but becoming F.I.E.R.C.E. allows us to know who we are, where you are going, and hold our head high due to having a renewed mind.

How to Become F.I.E.R.C.E.

Being F.I.E.R.C.E. is a mindset. It means you are focused and unstoppable. It means you will not allow anything or anyone

hinder you from being who God purposed and destined you to be. It means you understand your role in your household, the marketplace, and society. It means you are a transformational leader who things about necessary changes and creates a vision to execute change. It means you know who you are and Whose you are. You are #FIERCE #Unstoppable #PurposeDriven!

Once again, thank you for purchasing this book and making the choice to pour into yourself. Now, let's begin the process towards self-empowerment, healing, and self-love. The best is yet to come. Let's get F.I.E.R.C.E.!

Things Needed

This book
A mirror and some tissue
A journal and a pen
The truth
A heart willing to forgive
A new outlook on life

Although there are sections to write your responses in the book, you might want to have a personal journal in case you do not have enough room to write.

Journaling is a great way to express your thoughts, feelings, outlook, and plans. Always have your journal near you or record it on your cellular phone and journal it later.

WHO DO I TURN TO
(a poem about a turning point in life)

I cry, I scream, I hurt
Who hears me?
Who feels my pain?
Who can relate?
Who even wants to understand?
Who really cares?
I watch my life slip through my fingers
I watch everything be taken away from me
They laugh, they point, and they mock me
Some think I am crazy
Some think I am lazy
Some hate my existence
What happened?
What's really going on?
Who do I turn to?

Who can help me now?
Now one seems to care
I feel like I am trapped in a never-ending battle
A battle with my mind
With my life
With the church
With my family

When will all of this pain end?
When does my peace get restored?
When I cry, I scream because of the pain I have endured
When I scream, the sounds are ignored
When the pain comes upon me, it engulfs my soul
So quickly the pain overwhelms me
and creates a mass of confusion
I stood by so many people and they turned their back on me
It hurts, but now I see what kindness gets you - a broken heart
I sit here with eyes full of tears,
who really cares is what I want to know
Lonely, afraid, confused, dismayed
Who do I turn to?

My body is aching from this never-ending battle
Suddenly, I hear a voice that I have heard before
The Voice says, "Tell about what you are going through
For someone else is going through the same thing too
Tell how I brought you out of the valley
Into a land that you never knew before
Tell how I gave you the desires of your heart and so much more
I did it all because I love you
Deep down I know it's hard for you to believe Me
Because no one else loves you and they made you hate yourself
My child, I created you and have great plans for you
Just hold on because the anointing that I gave you is only for you
They won't understand you because
they don't want to relate to your pain

You will tell of heartaches, abandonment,
loneliness, abuse, and strife
You will tell how each incident violated your mind
You will tell them how I brought sunshine
in the midst of the storm
You will tell how you finally realized that
I loved you and I made you love yourself
The story you will tell is going to bless so many people
I had to send you through so you could
understand My love for you
I wanted you for Me and you put Me on a shelf
It's time to take Me off of the shelf and tell
this story to someone else
I hear you every time you cry and I will keep
My promise of making things better for you
But you have to keep the promise that you made to Me too
That you would tell My story throughout the land
I love you, My child and I want what is best for you
Just trust, believe, and know that I will never
leave you nor forsake you
And I will never put more on you than you can bear"

Who did I turn to?
I turned to God
For He is my refuge and very present help in the time of trouble!

• **Kimberly, 06/23/01©** •

FEARLESS

Hey, I know people like to get to the meat of a book and start at the first chapter, but if you have not read the Foreword, Preface, Introduction, and How to Use this Book chapters, please go back and read them before reading this chapter. Also, read the poem, Who Do I Turn To, preceding this chapter. There is a lot of great information in those sections that set the tone for reading this book. Trust me you will be glad you read those chapters before jumping into the first chapter. Each part of this book serves as a stepping stone; no skipping steps. #MuchLove

How Fear Became a Stronghold

"But of the tree of the knowledge of good and evil, thou shalt not eat of it: for in the day that thou eatest thereof thou shalt surely die"

• **Genesis 2:17, King James Version** •

Since the onset of sin, fear stepped on the scene when Adam and Eve disobeyed God by eating from the tree of knowledge of good and evil. The law of first mention of a form of fear is found in Genesis 3:10 (King James Version) which reads, "And he said, I heard thy voice in the garden, and I was afraid, because I was naked; and I hid myself." According to Blue Letter Bible, the word afraid in this Scripture is the Hebrew word yaré which means "to fear; causatively to frighten; be afraid; fearful."

A stronghold is a wrong or incorrect thinking pattern that has molded itself into our way of thinking. Strongholds have the capability to affect our feelings, how we respond to various situations in life, and our freedom. Strongholds can be hard to break because they grip our mind and change our thinking, perception, and mentality.

"For the weapons of our warfare are not carnal, but mighty through God to the pulling down of strong holds"

• 2 Corinthians 10:4, King James Version •

Fear is a stronghold that hinders our thoughts and inhibits our mental capabilities. Fear makes us think less than what we are capable of and cripples us. The time has come to get rid of fear and move boldly into our purpose. The time has come to take the limits off and excel in every aspect of our life.

What is fear?

The first strategy in the journey to live a F.I.E.R.C.E. lifestyle is to become fearless. In order to become fearless, we must first understand the meaning of fear. According to Google Dictionary, fear is defined as "an unpleasant emotion caused by the belief that someone or something is dangerous, likely to cause pain, or a threat" (noun); "be afraid of (someone or something) as likely to be dangerous, painful, or threatening" (verb). We often hear people state fear as an acronym meaning

False Evidence Appearing Real. Fear inhibits us from seeing things in a positive manner and makes us feel inferior.

Now, do not get me wrong. There will be times in life when fear is natural and there is nothing wrong with that. What I am referring to is no longer living in fear whereas it cripples us from walking in the promises of God, but instead living an exciting, purpose driven life that does not have constraints or limitations on our capabilities.

How does fear overtake us?

Oftentimes, we wonder how fear overtakes us and why we operate in a state of fear. We question our ability to be great. We question our ability for success. We doubt that we have potential and second guess our every move. Who told us we could not be great? Who told us we had to settle for less than what we are worth? Fear told us and we believed it. The question is why do we believe negative things that people say to us, and when someone speaks positively to us, we feel as though the truth is a lie?

Fear is one of the strongest mind games on this earth. Picture a tree. You are the trunk of the tree. The root and branches represent extensions of you and what you are dealing with/experiencing. Fear is the root of the tree and some of the branches of the tree are low self-esteem, comparison, and doubt. The branches (comparison, doubt, low self-esteem,

jealousy, envy) feed off of the root (fear). As the tree continues to grow due to the roots expanding and finding more nourishment, the roots begin to dig deep into the soil and the branches continue to flourish.

Like the tree, fear continues to feed off of our insecurities and jealousies, and as a result we develop strongholds that entangle us. The time has come for us to no longer allow fear to overtake our life. We accomplish this by cutting off and uprooting the source of our fear (the root). Once the root has been uprooted, the tree can no longer survive because its source of nourishment has been demolished. Who is ready to uproot their source of fear?

Life Story
The Power of Words

For years, I operated in the fear of success. Due to the hatred certain family members displayed towards me, I never wanted to be successful because I was afraid of what they would say about me. I was around 11 years old and my family members were telling me, "You think you are all that." I became fearful of what they would say to me if I became successful. I retreated and settled for ordinary, but deep inside I knew I was destined to be extraordinary.

Do you see how powerful words are and their ability to speak death or life? The Bible tells us "Death and life are in the power

of the tongue" (Proverbs 18:21, King James Version). My family members' words had a lasting effect on me that boggled my mind and tormented me for years. That is until the day I learned who I was, discovered my worth, and cut off the spirit of fear.

A Poem that Changed my Perspective

One day while watching the movie, Akeelah and the Bee, I was astonished at a poem the professor had Akeelah read aloud. The words in the poem were so powerful that I searched the Internet to find the poem. The poem is entitled Our Deepest Fear by Marianne Williamson.

Our Deepest Fear

> Our deepest fear is not that we are inadequate.
> Our deepest fear is that we are powerful beyond measure.
> It is our light, not our darkness
> That most frightens us.
>
> We ask ourselves
> Who am I to be brilliant, gorgeous, talented, fabulous?
> Actually, who are you not to be?
>
> You are a child of God.
> Your playing small
> Does not serve the world.
> There's nothing enlightened about shrinking
> So that other people won't feel insecure around you.
>
> We are all meant to shine,
> As children do.

We were born to make manifest
The glory of God that is within us.

It's not just in some of us;
It's in everyone.

And as we let our own light shine,
We unconsciously give other people permission to do the same.
As we're liberated from our own fear,
Our presence automatically liberates others.

Note: This inspiring poem is from Marianne Williamson's book, A Return to Love

The questions the professor asked Akeelah after she read the poem are what made this part of the movie so profound to me.

> Professor: "What does it mean?"
> Akeelah: "I don't know. That I'm not supposed to be afraid."
> Professor: "Afraid of what?"
> Akeelah: "Afraid of … me."

When I read the poem in its entirety, tears began to flow from my eyes. I was astonished at the writer's words, how she captured my thoughts and feelings, and the sense of empowerment I received from reading the poem. No longer did I have to settle for less or operate at my minimized potential. No longer did I have to be afraid to be me. Thank you, Marianne Williamson, for giving me a piece of my life back. This poem helped me recognize fearful areas in my life. I have my mentees read this is poem as a method to get to the root of the fear that is crippling

them so I can incorporate techniques that will help them overcome fear and walk in their purpose.

When I read this poem, I had a thought provoking moment in which I realized our deepest fear is not what others have done or will do to us. Our deepest fear is being afraid to be ourselves and exerting the power that is within us. We operate in a less than mentality so others will not feel bad or tease us. This is what I had been doing my entire life and it was time for a new attitude and a new perspective for my life. The time had come to change the status quo of my life. But how could I do that? The first step of my journey of discovering self-empowerment was to overcome fear. I finally realized it was okay for me to be myself and that belittling who I was to appease others was destroying my happiness. All of that changed when I learned the strategies of living a F.I.E.R.C.E. lifestyle.

Overcoming years of self-hatred

Honestly, before I could overcome fear, I had to learn to love myself. The hatred and jealousy my family had towards me made me hate myself. I never saw my life as valuable and I was usually depressed. The road to learning to love myself was very long. I hated my forehead, voice, nose, appearance, and me. How can you love someone that you hate? How do you value something that you do not know the value of?

Self-hatred is a scar that many people wear and the world can

make this scar feel like a continuous open wound someone is pouring salt on. The world judges people based on their perception of how they think people should be instead of allowing people to be themselves. The world sees someone's hurt and administers agony along with that person's pain.

Oftentimes, I shielded myself from others hurting me by saying, "My own family does not like me. So, why would I care if you liked me?" This verbiage and mentality helped me cope with rejection and hurt, but deep down I was longing to be loved and accepted. Soon, hearing the words "I love you" became an entryway to my heart and my soul. If a guy told me he loved me, he had won my heart. I love you were also the words that began to torment my soul because those guys' love was only a temporary fix for what I longed for. These men could not love me how I longed, needed, or deserved to be loved. My heart yearned for affirmation and acceptance; while their love was words based on their own personal desire. My ears heard what they longed to hear (I love you), but my heart never experienced what it needed to feel (someone who genuinely cared about me, not expecting anything in return).

I learned people often used the words "I love you" without much emotion because those words could be used to gain access into forbidden areas. Once I stopped yearning to hear I love you, my perception changed because I knew I had to learn to love me in order for someone to love me how I deserved to be

loved. Learning to love myself gave me time to heal and become prepared for the man who has shown me the love I deserve.

I used to always question why certain family members did not like me. My mother would ask me, "Why does that bother you so much?" I did not have an answer to her question, but it hurt me deeply that they did not like me or love me. I often wondered what I did to them. The only answer I had was ... I was born. For this reason, I began to question my existence and hated myself even more.

One day out of the blue, my cousin said to me, "It was not that I did not like you when we were growing up. It was because you had something I did not have – a father." My cousin's words were confirmation of what God had told me. My heart smiled that day and it was as if I received a piece of my identity back.

There Is No Fear in FIERCE

(F.I.E.R.C.E. Women's Empowerment Movement logo created by Digital Art and Design by Veronica Nicole)

When you look into the tiger's eyes, what do you see? I see eyes that are focused, purpose driven, and fierce. I see eyes that exhibit no fear. The eye of the tiger is often referred to as feeling confident. When a tiger fixes its eye on its prey, the tiger is focused, confident, and is not afraid to capture what it sets its eyes upon.

From re-seraching the tiger I learned, there is no fear in fierce. And that, in order to walk in my purpose, I had to become focused and fearless. Writing this book was a moment of stepping outside of my comfort zone and fulfilling what God told me to do. Sharing portions of my life story brought back memories that I had to address, confront, and be delivered from. I had to realize my past did not dictate my future, and although I had made numerous mistakes, God still graced me with life in order to get things right and walk in my purpose. My research on the tiger made me understand the importance of being unstoppable and going after what was mine. No longer would I stand on the sidelines being boring and merely exisitng. It was time to live life and be F.I.E.R.C.E.

As we read, fear entangles our mind and has us feeling vulnerable. I want you to know you are victorious. No longer shall you be a victim, but instead, you will be victorius in every aspect of your life. For years, you may have felt like you were walking around with blinders on that kept you in a zone of only looking at particular things. Well, today the blinders are being

removed. Go ahead stretch your neck and look around. There is so much for you to see and experience. There is no need to be afraid. "Greater is he that is in you, than he that is in the world" (1 John 4:4, King James Version). When we operate in a fearful state, we confine our mind and abilities. It is time to live and explore life not being confined by fear.

What is your greatest aspiration? What have you put on the back burner that needs to be completed? What is stopping you from fulfilling your dreams and walking in your purpose? What are you afraid of? There is no fear in **F.I.E.R.C.E.** Journal your answers here…

_____
_____
_____
_____
_____
_____
_____
_____
_____
_____
_____
_____
_____

What controls your fears – a poem

Whatcha 'fraid of?

Whatcha 'fraid of?
The thought of another taking control of who you've become
Someone that comes along and interrupts your comfort zone
The one that seems so right
But you're afraid of another holding you tight

Whatcha 'fraid of?
The stares and the glares
The feeling that no one really cares
The thought of being hurt again
The feeling of not having a close friend

Whatcha 'fraid of?
Losing the last piece of your heart
Not knowing the time to make a new start
Thinking no one cares about you at all
You're finally up, and scared once again you might fall

Whatcha 'fraid of?
Trusting someone after everyone has stolen all you have
Been hurt time and time and time again, you do the math
Bound in your mind for so long
Weeping, crying, and singing silly love songs

Whatcha 'fraid of?
Overcoming a fear that has kept you stifled for years
Hiding behind your hands and your tears
Opening up to a new beginning
Still not knowing why the other one is ending

Whatcha 'fraid of?
Actually being loved

Love sent from Heaven above
Love so real is seems wrong
Love that your heart has longed

Whatcha 'fraid of?!

For a season in my life, I was afraid of me. I shielded my face and my heart from the world. Not wanting to be recognized or noticed. I stayed in the comfort zone of my own little world I created. It was comfortable there. No need to come out and be hurt by the world or deceived by the motives of others. I was content. So I thought.

After several abusive relationships, my heart felt so heavy and I thought I'd never heal from the pain. It hurt so much that I just stayed to myself and never wanted to really love again. Know that fear is of the devil. In God's timing, healing and deliverance will come forth. God will restore you, and you will be whole and complete lacking nothing. Don't be 'fraid! Stay prayerful! Embrace your newness, and your new beginning, for old things have passed away. God is doing a NEW thing in you, for you, and through you.

• **Kimberly, 05/08/2006©** •

Steps for getting to the root of fear
Identify what you are afraid of?

What are you afraid of? Why are you retreating instead of pressing forward in your purpose? What has been spoken over your life that has your mind entangled in a web of lies that are rooted in fear?

The first step of overcoming fear is to identify what you are afraid of. I pose the question to you again ... what are you afraid of? Write your response here...

_____
_____
_____
_____
_____
_____
_____
_____
_____
_____
_____
_____
_____
_____

Research what you are afraid of

Now that you have identified what you are afraid of, the second step of overcoming fear is to research what you are afraid of. For example, if your fear is rejection, you would research rejection. Researching your fear(s) will equip you to understand the root of your fear (rejection) and identify the branches associated with the fear (for example: abandonment, loneliness).

See, we cannot just cut off fear without cutting off the things that were feeding our fear(s). This is why certain seminars are temporary quick fixes that motivate us for the moment because we are not able to move forward due to fear and other baggage. My goal is to get to the root of your fear(s) and expose what it is feeding off of. We are going to destroy every part of the tree, including the root so fear cannot grow again. Then, when you attend another seminar, the techniques and information provided will stick because you eliminated yourself of the unnecessary baggage that was hindering your ability to be receptive.

List definitions and research about your fear(s) here...

_____
_____
_____
_____
_____
_____
_____
_____
_____
_____
_____
_____
_____
_____
_____
_____
_____
_____
_____
_____

Feed your Faith

The third step of overcoming fear is to find Scriptures to combat your fear(s) so you can feed your faith. Scriptures are a great source of nutrients to empower and strengthen you. Find Scriptures related to overcoming fear as well as the sources that are feeding your fear(s).

A great Scripture about the spirit of fear is "For God hath not given us the spirit of fear; but of power, and of love, and of a sound mind" (2 Timothy 1:7, King James Version). Power provides strength, love conquers fear, and a sound mind does not subject to the norm. God gave us power, love, and a sound mind to rid the spirit of fear. During this process, we will help you get your power back, love yourself again, and establish a sound mind.

Write your Scriptures to combat fear here…

Renewing your mind

> *"And be not conformed to this world: but be ye transformed by the renewing of your mind, that ye may prove what is that good, and acceptable, and perfect, will of God"*
>
> • Romans 12:2, King James Version •

According to Blue Letter Bible, in this verse, transform is a Greek word: metamorphoo which means to transfigure or change. This is where the word metamorphosis derives from.

From the Blue Letter Bible, in this verse, renew is a Greek word: anakainosis which means renovation, renewal, complete change for the better. It is important that we transform your mentality by renewing your mind. We will change the way you think by renovating your thought process.

Do you recall the television show, Extreme Makeover: Home Edition? Due to an unexpected hardship, the architects and designers of the television show would transform and renew a family's home. Along with the home makeover, the team would provide the family with a new sense of hope. Well, we are going to conduct an Extreme Transformation: You Edition. Remember before I talked about ridding yourself of stinking thinking (negative thoughts)? Yes, we are going to change your negative mentality into a positive mentality by changing how you think and speak.

Remember in school we were taught a negative plus a negative

equals a positive? And two back-to-back negatives in a sentence made what you said positive? Well, all of the negative occurrences you have encountered are about to be transformed so you can live a positive rewarding life. This is not to say what you have gone through does not hurt or that it will take a moment for you to heal. Our focus is to change your perspective which will eventually change your outlook.

For example: My love life has been full of heartbreaks due to cheating and abusive behavior. For 15 years, I left the dating scene and took time to myself where I reflected on my past and prepared for my future. During that time, I changed my view of relationships, because at first, I never wanted to date again or get married due to the heartbreaks I had endured. Eventually, I dated again, and the relationship did not work. At first, I was hurt, but then, I realized this had nothing to do with me, my purpose, or exploring love again. This served as a reason and a test of my fears. I would often say my fear was being forgotten and hurt.

Even though I was hurt, it was not the root of my fear because I know being hurt is a part of life. Knowing who I am and what I deserve along with having self-love kept me focused as to what I will and will not tolerate from anyone. I have come too far to allow certain things to weigh me down or get me off course. This served as a test and I thank God for changing my mentality and for making me F.I.E.R.C.E. Yes, what made me love me was

overcoming fear, learning to love myself, and not settling for less than I deserve.

Daily Affirmations

The Word of God says, "Thou shalt also decree a thing, and it shall be established unto thee" (Job 22:28). For the next three (3) days, I want you to speak the list of affirmations (listed below) over your life several times a day. Post the list everywhere. Every morning and every night I want you to look at yourself in the mirror and recite the affirmations. Look yourself in the eyes when you recite each affirmation. You are going to speak to the woman lying dormant within you and awaken her.

I even want you to text yourself certain affirmations throughout the day. Post the affirmations on your social media page. (When posting your affirmations, please include the hashtag #WWMLM.)

We are going to get you to love on you and spend time pouring into you. Cutting off the root of fear can only be done by finding true love for yourself because it is the lack of self-love that had you believing those lies and being bound by fear in the first place.

I am beautiful.
I am successful.
I am smart.
I am a lender and not a borrower.
I am above and not beneath.
I am wealthy.
I am on the road to discovering my identity and love for self.
I love me.
I am not the lies that have been spoken over me.
I will no longer walk in fear.
I am not a failure.
I am Fearless.
I, (your name), am a success story – not a tragedy.

Reflection

How did you feel stating the affirmations? Was it hard looking at yourself in the mirror? Were you being truthful and transparent? Journal and reflect on the experience here.

_____

_____

_____

_____

_____

_____

_____

_____

_____

_____

_____

_____

_____

LIFE APPLICATION:
What are you going to do to break through your glass ceiling to become fearless?

In this section, journal what you will do to detach from the spirit of fear.

It is time to put what we have discussed and what you journaled into action. This will become your action plan as you prepare and apply what you have learned to receive your break through from the spirit of fear.

_____
_____
_____
_____
_____
_____
_____
_____
_____
_____

Fearless Prayer

Father, I thank You today that You have not given me the spirit of fear, but a sound mind is what You have given me. I thank you that I walk in boldness and have no fear. I thank you that You made me strong and I am created for great purpose. I know, Lord, that I will not be afraid of ten thousands of people who have set themselves against me roundabout, but I walk in the strength that You have given me. So Lord, this day, continue to give me strength in those things that I can see and cannot see. I know that the joy of the Lord is my strength. I thank You that I am fearfully and wonderfully made and fear does not dwell here or within me. I walk in the abundance of all that You have in store for me and I say Hallelujah. I rise up in authority this day and forever. Amen

INNOVATIVE

What does innovative mean?

The second strategy of the journey to live a F.I.E.R.C.E. lifestyle is to become innovative. According to Google Dictionary, innovative is defined as "(of a person) introducing new ideas; original and creative in thinking." Innovation and creativity can be new or by transforming and refining something previously created. We find this all the time with technology and education. No matter what, the world will continue to evolve. Technology cannot be stopped. So, why not make it so you are a contributing factor to what evolves?

I am not a creative person so how can I be innovative or become innovative?

Do not allow the word creative to intimidate you. We are all creative. Have you read the book of Genesis? "In the beginning God created the heaven and the earth" (Genesis 1:1, King James Version). Let's scroll down a little further: "So God created man in his own image, in the image of God created he him; male and female created he them" (Genesis 1:27, King James Version). Wow, God created you in His image; so that means you have the power to create things as well. According to Blue Letter Bible, in these Scriptures, create is a Hebrew word: bara which means to shape, form, something new, birth, new conditions and

circumstances, and transformation. Creativity lies within you. The time has come to birth and make something new.

People tend to think they are not creative because they do not understand creativity happens in various forms. Usually we relate creativity to art, but it can be writing, poetry, carpentry, drawing, painting, cooking, baking, acting, dancing, singing, comedy, consulting, designing, photography, graphic design, teaching, engineering, pottery, and so much more. You are creative. We just have to discover what it is that you like doing and use that as the foundation to build upon.

Now, do you see why the first strategy for living a F.I.E.R.C.E. lifestyle was to uproot fear and renew our mind from negative thinking? It is important that we understand our thoughts shape what we become as well as what we create. Remember, death and life are in the power of the tongue. No longer will you say you are not creative, but instead you will say I am creative. "I can't" will no longer be a part of your vocabulary. I want you to memorize the following Scripture:

> *"I can do all things through Christ which strengtheneth me"*
> • Philippians 4:13, King James Version •

Life story
Recognizing my creative side

Years ago, my previous supervisor helped me tap into a new realm of creativity that I never knew existed in me or considered to be a form of creativity. When my supervisor needed a report to look a certain way, she would contact me because I would make it colorful and comprehensive; whereas my co-worker would throw something together and present it.

The Word of God says, "And whatsoever ye do, do it heartily, as to the Lord, and not unto men" (Colossians 3:23, King James Version). With that in mind, when I am working on something, I operate in a Spirit of excellence by giving the project my all because my work and my life are representations of God. One day my supervisor told me, "One word to describe you would be creative", and she began to tell me how and why she described me as being creative. I thank her for helping me understand the essence and art of creativity, and not to limit myself to thinking creativity was only a certain way.

Learning a new way to teach

Let's fast forward a few years. When I was in Teacher's Training Course at my previous church, I tested high as analytical being my primary learning style and scored evenly with the other three learning styles: dynamic, imaginative, and common sense. Learning styles refer to how a person

receives, understands, comprehends, and organizes information. Analytical learners prefer organized, orderly information, and they like things straight to the point without any fluff. Dynamic learners see a broad picture and bring in illustrations to help deliver their message. Imaginative learners tell stories with their message. Common sense learners do not want to hear a lot of talk, but instead like hands-on activities and real-life scenarios. Which of these learning styles do you think is your prominent learning style?

In our teacher's training course, we needed to know our learning style to show us how we would prominently teach, because people tend to teach how they comprehend information. But, in the teacher's training course, we were taught to teach in a manner that incorporates all four learning styles so no one felt left out when we are teaching the lesson.

One day my teacher told me she wanted me to start operating in the dynamic learning style because it was in me. Honestly, this was a stretch for me, but I accepted the challenge. To my surprise, learning to operate in the dynamic learning style opened a whole new realm for me. Not just with teaching, but with every aspect of my life. Stepping outside of the box (the norm) and learning a new concept birthed a new sense of creativity within me and I was excited!

Honestly, I might have tested high as an analytical learner, but I do not like being taught using that style especially if the

teacher has a monotone voice nor do I like teaching in only that style. Yup, I have always been different. LOL I always felt that teaching is an art that should be taught with passion using illustrations and stories so it captures the learners' attention. Although my career field is not teaching (at the moment), teaching is my passion.

Applying creativity to everyday life

Since overcoming the fear of failure, I take more risks and love learning. I used to be afraid of tests and reading due to having a reading comprehension difficulty, but I loved learning as long as reading was not involved. I figured why try and process information if I was going to forget it after I read it. I tackled the fear of reading by teaching myself how to learn how my brain comprehends and retains information. Now, I am working towards my Doctoral degree. Once again, God took a fear and turned it around for good.

In my spare time, I love creating invitations and fliers for events. My daughter and I assist people with event planning as a way to be a blessing to others. Oftentimes, I will revise résumés, write and design obituaries, or edit documents for people. Eventually, I want to learn web design and Photoshop for fun. I learned how to work a film camera and direct from volunteering at my previous church. I became a radio personality out of curiosity of how the equipment worked. My point is you never

stop growing and do not be afraid to learn something new. Remember the story about the talents? I want you to exercise, utilize, and grow what God has given you and placed within you. You do God a disservice when you do not cultivate the gifts/talents He gave you.

*I am learning all I can in this season to be
all God has called me to be forever.*

• **Kimberly Rashawn** •

Techniques for recognizing your creativity
Make a list of things that you like to do.

_____

_____

_____

_____

_____

_____

_____

_____

_____

_____

_____

_____

_____

_____

_____

_____

_____

_____

Now, I want you to look at what you wrote. The section is not blank, right? Aha, you have the power to create. Now, we will refine the list as to how you can be creative with what you like to do by writing how you can exercise and utilize your talents and gifts.

For example: If you like to bake, you can be creative by baking cookies or cakes as birthday presents. Mrs. Fields' Cookies was established due to Mrs. Fields baking cookies for her husband's co-workers. Someone told the husband how good the product was, and the next thing you know it was a franchise that has been sold. I have a friend who makes some awesome cupcakes. Now, her cupcakes are sold in a local restaurant. Your gift will make room for you. Stop thinking you are not good enough.

Now, do you see how what you like doing can become a stream of income or a way to bless others? Everyone has creativity within them because we were created in God's image and God created the heavens and the earth. It just takes a moment to connect the dots and realize what God has placed within you. Yes, what made me love me was realizing my potential and creativity.

Transparent Moment: In the final stages of writing this book, I stopped writing and editing the final manuscript. Life became overwhelming because I thought what I had written was not good enough. I kept saying I will finish it, but would find other things to do besides sit at my computer to make the edits.

One day God said, "I believe in you. Why don't you believe in yourself?" God's words really touched me and gave me the spark I needed. So much had been invested in this book and I had to use the talent that was given and cast fear to the side in order to bring God's vision to fruition.

"You are never too old to set another goal or to dream a new dream."
• **Les Brown** •

Expound on how you can exercise your talents (things you like to do) in this section…

_____

_____

_____

_____

_____

_____

_____

_____

_____

_____

_____

_____

_____

_____

_____

_____

Daily affirmations

Your list is expanding. Here is your new list of affirmations to recite daily.

I am beautiful.
I am successful.
I am smart.
I am a lender and not a borrower.
I am above and not beneath.
I am wealthy.
I am on the road to discovering my identity and love for self.
I love me.
I am not the lies that have been spoken over me.

I will no longer walk in fear.
I am not a failure.
I am creative.
I, (your name), am a success story – not a tragedy.
I am Fearless.
I am Innovative.

Reflection

How did you feel stating the affirmations? Was it hard looking at yourself in the mirror? Were you being truthful and transparent? Journal and reflect on the experience here.

_____

_____

_____

_____

_____

_____

_____

_____

_____

_____

_____

_____

_____

_____

_____

LIFE APPLICATION:
*What are you going to do to break through your glass
ceiling to be innovative and utilize your creativity?*

In this section, journal what you will do to utilize your creativity.

It is time to put what we have discussed and what you journaled into action. This will become your action plan as you prepare and apply what you have learned to be more creative and walk in your purpose.

_____

_____

_____

_____

_____

_____

_____

_____

_____

Innovative Prayer

Oh Father, I thank You that You have created me before the foundation of the world, and You blew Your breath into me and gave me life. You created me, Lord, for great purpose and sent Your Son who died on the cross for me and saved me so that old things are passed away and I am made new. In You, I live, move, and have my being. In You, Lord, I can move from the old to the new for You said, "Behold, I am doing a new thing" and I thank You. I am chosen, a royal priesthood, a holy nation, and a people for Your own possession proclaiming the Excellencies of Him that has called me out of darkness into His marvelous light. So now, I put on the new and step into all You have for me. New realms! New destiny! New purpose! New doors! New ideas and inventions! I step into them now, Lord! Amen

EMPOWERED

What does empowered mean?

The third strategy of the journey to live a F.I.E.R.C.E. lifestyle is to become empowered. This book will focus on self-empowerment. According to Google Dictionary, empowerment is defined as "make (someone) stronger and more confident, especially in controlling their life and claiming their rights." I love this definition! This definition is so on point, not only for living a F.I.E.R.C.E. lifestyle, but also for living an empowered lifestyle.

What is different about this book that will empower me?

You are different. Your level of expectancy has changed. You are seeking something new from God. And guess what?! This is your season to receive your breakthrough in so many areas of your life! You do not realize how excited I am about your future. I love empowering others for change.

The main thing I want you to realize is – this is a process. The things that occurred in your life did not happen overnight, so it will take a minute to remove the layers of hurt as well as the weight of life that is stacked upon your shoulders.

Now, do not get me wrong by thinking that you will be walking

around smiling all of the time and just so happy; although you could. But, life happens and sometimes things catch us off guard. After going through these strategies, you will be equipped and empowered to react differently to life's obstacles because these strategies will have your 'come back' game stronger than it was before. You will have a new perspective of how you view, approach, and overcome things.

Every process begins with a new perspective

Earlier, we talked about renewing our mind. Let's dig into that process a little more.

> *"And be not conformed to this world: but be ye transformed by the renewing of your mind, that ye may prove what is that good, and acceptable, and perfect, will of God"*
>
> • Romans 12:2, King James Version •

It is so important that we begin to think differently and speak life to our situations. Our faith has to be strengthened and worked like a muscle. After hearing years of 'you are stupid', 'you can't', or 'you are going to fail', it takes the mind a minute to overcome and reprogram itself from the negativity it heard and believed during that time, and in some cases adapted itself accordingly. For this reason, we need to understand how powerful words are. This is why daily affirmations are so important. Affirmations empower and strengthen us; they are like weights to tone and

sculpt our mind. When we recite positive affirmations, our mind begins to reprogram itself from what it once believed to be true. The process of renewing your mind will lead to a permanent, positive change.

When we change how we think, our perception changes. We begin to see things differently. Our mind opens to a whole new realm. Renewing your mind and speaking positively is a rewarding experience.

Have you ever encountered a situation in which someone down talked you and made you feel inferior? How did that make you feel? Were you empowered after that experience?

I had a supervisor who never had anything nice to say about me. When I asked why I was not advancing within department, I was told a degrading, untruthful response. Initially, after my supervisor's remarks, I felt defeated, but then I realized and became determined what this person thought of me would not become my opinion of myself. More importantly, I made sure I held onto my values and would not allow this to make me bitter or torn. I knew God had better in store for me, and this path along my life journey was a learning experience. Know this … sometimes bad experiences we encounter are for us to learn how not to treat others.

Implementing a New Perspective can be Empowering

Recently, I needed to make choices regarding the things I was eating to lead a healthier lifestyle. I had a choice of possibly being on medication or changing my eating habits. I began to research foods to avoid and read food labels before making a purchase. I joined a training program, which gave me the jumpstart I needed to lose weight. All of these processes empowered me to do things differently.

When I returned to the doctor, I received a good report. Now, I am going to kick it into another gear. I empowered my mind by researching information to make healthier choices. I had to understand my body was a temple and I needed to stop defiling my temple. I understood the power I would gain by making better choices in various aspects of my life. Changing my view of food and my eating habits were a rewarding experience. I am looking forward to the new, sculpted, and toned me (from the inside out).

We have the power of knowledge and information at our fingertips via the Internet. We can receive numerous resources within seconds. What is it that you need to do to jumpstart your life to live an empowered lifestyle? What is holding you back from changing the status quo of your life? Write your answers here…

_____

_____

_____

_____

_____

_____

_____

_____

_____

_____

_____

_____

_____

Life story

I am a radio personality of a broadcast called The Empowerment Hour. My main goal for starting the broadcast was to empower people to walk in their purpose and to promote other people's ministries and work. Initially, I tussled with hosting the broadcast and came up with every reason imaginable as to why I could not host the program. Guess what? The reasons were actually excuses and I finally agreed to host the broadcast once I realized this was a part of my purpose.

Honestly, there was an inkling of fear that was trying to set in. I never thought my voice exercised much power, but God had to show me the different platforms He placed me on in the past and how He was enlarging my territory for greater works for His glory. I began to cry and repented. Isn't that just like God to use what we do not like about our self to give Him glory? Moses did not feel as though he was an adequate speaker because he stuttered, but God used Him to speak to Pharaoh to deliver His people from Egypt (read Exodus 4). God takes what we consider a negative and turns it into a positive. From this I learned, it does not matter how I see myself; what really matters is how God sees me.

My calling and purpose are not tied to my own hopes and desires; they are tied to what God has purposed and called me to do. It is not about me, which is the main reason I wrote this book. My purpose is to empower others, and God is giving me different platforms to declare His glory.

> *"And I will make of thee a great nation, and I will bless thee, and make thy name great; and thou shalt be a blessing"*
>
> • Genesis 12:2, King James Version •

Overcoming fear allowed me to be receptive to what God was doing in, around, and through me. The main thing was for me to be obedient to His will and not my own desires (obedience is better than sacrifice). Again, do you see why the first strategy of overcoming fear was so important? If I had not overcome fear, I would not have recognized when fear was attempting to raise its head to deter me from what I was called and purposed to do.

Strategies for renewing your mind and becoming empowered

In the 1990s, there was a song entitled "Free Your Mind" by En Vogue that I loved. Part of the chorus says, "Free your mind and the rest will follow." This is so true. When we free our mind of negative thought patterns, we are receptive of positive thought patterns. Thus, this is part of the formula of renewing your mind. We have to free our mind of the things that are entangling us and keeping us bound.

I want you to envision yourself inside of a box. Now, I want you to envision the box filled with things you have heard or seen that have discouraged and hurt you. How are you reacting to being inside the box with these items? Are you uncomfortable

being in the box? This is how your mind is reacting to the negativity that you have been hearing and thinking. Your mind is uncomfortable. Now, I want you to envision yourself breaking out of the box. How are you reacting to being outside of the box? When we rid ourselves of the negative experiences we have heard, thought, and/or encountered, we free our mind of the things that have been entangling it. Yes, what made me love me was overcoming the negative voices that said I would never be anything and empowering myself to fulfill my dreams and walk in my purpose.

Ridding Yourself of Negativity Spoken Over Your Life

Over the years, people have said things to you that have discouraged you. This next exercise might be a little difficult at first, but I want you to press your way through it.

Grab a sheet a paper that is not in a journal. I want you to write every negative thing someone has spoken to you on the sheet of paper. Also, write every negative thing you have said to yourself or thought about yourself.

I do not want you to write it in this book or your journal because once you are finished writing the list, you will denounce every word that has been spoken against you, rip the paper into small pieces and throw it in the trash or flush it down the toilet. You will say the prayer below while tearing up the paper.

Recite this prayer while tearing up the paper...

I come against every negative word that has been spoken to me and over my life. I speak to every dead and desolate area of my life. I am not the negative things people have said to me or about me. I am not a failure, tragedy, regret, or loser. I have a sound mind and a renewed mind. No longer shall the things of my past hinder me or make me feel less than. Thank You, Lord, that as I tear up this paper, I disconnect myself from every negative thing that has been said to me, thought, and/or spoken over me. Thank You, Lord, that my mind is being renewed and You are making all things new with me this very second. Amen.

Getting rid of the paper makes it so you cannot go back to it. Now, walk in your freedom and no longer allow negative words to have power over you.

Daily affirmations

Your list of daily affirmations is expanding. Here is a new list. Recite for the next three days.

I am beautiful.
I am successful.
I am smart.
I am a lender and not a borrower.
I am above and not beneath.
I am wealthy.

I am on the road to discovering my identity and love for self.
I love me.
I am not the lies that have been spoken over me.
I will not believe the lies others have said to me.
I will no longer walk in fear.
I am not a failure.
I am creative.
I am renewing my mind.
I am victorious.
I, (your name), am a success story – not a tragedy.
I am Fearless.
I am Innovative.
I am Empowered.

Reflection

How did you feel stating the affirmations? Was it hard looking at yourself in the mirror? Were you being truthful and transparent? Journal and reflect on the experience here...

_____
_____
_____
_____
_____
_____
_____
_____
_____
_____
_____
_____
_____

LIFE APPLICATION:
What are you going to do to break through your glass ceiling to stay empowered?

In this section, journal what you will do to stay empowered.

It is time to put what we have discussed and what you journaled into action. This will become your action plan as you prepare and apply what you have learned to receive your break through.

_____

_____

_____

_____

_____

_____

_____

_____

_____

_____

_____

Empowered Prayer

Father, I pray unto You today and ask that You hear Your servant's cry. I thank You that I am unshakeable, unmovable, and always abounding in the work of the Lord. You chose me for greatness and I am strong in everything that I do. You have placed many things in my hands that I know I can only do through you. I am empowered to take on and conquer new realms in the earth. I am forever qualified to do what You placed in my hands because you called me before the foundation of the world. I say that I am not weak, but strong. I am even being empowered to write the vision and make it plain as a means of empowering myself and others. I am even being empowered to go before kings and queens for Your glory. I am being empowered to go across mountains and valleys to reach your people. Thank You, Lord, for empowering and renewing my mind. Amen.

RESILIENT

What does resilient mean?

The fourth strategy of the journey to live a F.I.E.R.C.E. lifestyle is to become resilient. According to Google Dictionary, resilient is defined as "(of a person or animal) able to withstand or recover quickly from difficult conditions." When I look at this definition, I think of being fireproof. Years ago, there was a song called Something Inside So Strong by Labi Siffre that speaks of resilience and strength. A few lyrics to the song are:

> *"Something inside so strong.*
> *I know that I can make it*
> *Tho' you're doing me wrong, so wrong.*
> *You thought that my pride was gone.*
> *Oh no, something inside so strong."*

Even in times of tests and tribulations, there is something inside of us that is strong and wants to break free and will not be defeated.

One of my favorite Scriptures speaks of how God will make us stronger after we gone through for a while. Know that your tests and trials are not unnoticed and during those times, God's grace is sufficient for you.

⁸ Be sober, be vigilant; because your adversary the devil, as a roaring lion, walketh about, seeking whom he may devour: ⁹ Whom resist stedfast in the faith, knowing that the same afflictions are accomplished in your brethren that are in the world. ¹⁰ But the God of all grace, who hath called us unto his eternal glory by Christ Jesus, after that ye have suffered a while, make you perfect, stablish, strengthen, settle you

• 1 Peter 5:8-10, King James Version •

Is your 'comeback game' strong?

When difficult things occur in your life, how long does it take you to recover from the experience? I know it usually depends on the situation as to how long it might take you to recover. Depending on the level of difficulty, it might be a few minutes, hours, one day, or a few days for me to bounce back. The duration of time depends on how intense I think about what occurred and whether I need to find resolution to the occurrence.

Honestly, some situations have taken me years to recover from. Well, that was before I learned the strategies of living a F.I.E.R.C.E. lifestyle. In the past, I would dismiss or put things on the back burner instead of dealing with them. Now, I reflect, journal, put things in perspective, deal with it, pray, and move forward knowing I can come back from anything, especially with God as my strength and refuge. When we turn things over to God and let Him handle it, it makes things less difficult.

"God is our refuge and strength, a very present help in trouble"
• **Psalms 46:1, King James Version** •

With difficulties that are not very extreme, my come back game is pretty strong. Comeback game means to come back strong. Now, even if it has taken me years to recover, when I finally come back, my comeback game is still strong because I am no longer bound and I am stronger than I was before. Know this … the level of intensity of the difficult situation and how we comeback is different for everyone. I want to encourage you to not allow things to destroy you because that is an attack of the enemy.

Before God spoke F.I.E.R.C.E. into my life, my past was tormenting me. I did not have control over the situation or the outcome, but the effects of it were tormenting me. Instead of me controlling it, it was controlling me. I knew this had to change, but did not know how. It was not that I could not come back; I did not want to come back. Instead of being hurt again, I decided to live within my self-made bubble and behind my wall. As I said before I was merely existing – not living. This was not a part of God's plan or purpose for my life. He allowed me to dwell in my pity stage for a season, and when it was time for change, He ordered my steps. I am so glad I was obedient to follow His directive because becoming F.I.E.R.C.E. has literally changed my life.

Life story

Lost my value of life

When I was around 20 or 21, I was so sad and hated my life. One day I decided to commit suicide. The plan was to take two pills then increase the dosage every hour. After taking the second dosage (four pills within an hour), I felt weird. I began to cry because I thought about how my parents and my Granny would feel if I committed suicide. At that moment, although I did not value my own life, I valued their lives and did not want to put them through that pain. I called a friend and she talked me out of taking any more pills. Then I called the triage nurse to see if I needed to go to the hospital.

Oftentimes, I reflect on how I felt that day whereas I wanted to end my life and thank God for sparing me. I have hit some bumpy roads since then, but never to the point that I wanted to end my life. Thank You, Lord, for a renewed mind to understand the value of life.

If for any reason you are feeling depleted, depressed, and not valued or considering life is not worth living, please contact the suicide hotline to speak with someone. Your life does have purpose and you can make it past how you are currently feeling. Please do not give up.

National Suicide Prevention Hotline 1-800-273-8255

Devalued and unappreciated

During another season in my life, one of my previous supervisors always said negative things to me and made me feel like crap. The working environment was hostile and I was miserable. When I left the job and found other employment, I was still in a mode of feeling devalued and unappreciated. The years of verbal abuse had taken its toll on me, and even though this person was no longer my supervisor, the words they said were still effecting me. Since I had been in a verbally abusive relationship before, I knew the sting and power of words. I was still bound by the fear of words and actions of those in supervisory roles over me once I was in my new position. It took me a few years to regain my strength and come back from that experience once I was free. Although my comeback game took a little longer, I was stronger in the long run and learned how to professionally exercise my voice instead of retreating and hiding.

Getting past the hurt of the past and life's obstacles

Over the years, I have been in several abusive relationships (verbal, physical, financial, emotional, and Spiritual abuse). Sometimes I used to wonder what was wrong with me because I kept attracting men who eventually exerted some form of abuse or cheated on me. At one point, I began to get even with those who hurt me, and for a minute I had promised myself to be ruthless and heartless to those who had inflected pain upon me. This once shy, sweet, naïve girl was now a bad, bitter chick who was not taking anyone's ill behavior anymore. Deep down I

wanted revenge against those who afflicted pain upon me.

My ex-boyfriend's homie stepped to me so I talked to him, even though he had a girlfriend, I decided to become the side chick. Left him alone, and went back with my ex-boyfriend who was now with the girl he was cheating on me with, and regained my status as the main chick. I pulled knives out to protect myself from my abusers. I cursed out and belittled my verbal abuser in a manner that brought him to tears. I fought back when I was hit, knocked things off of dressers, and got out of moving cars. After a while, I began to do things without emotion because revenge was my motivation. My mind wanted to make others feel how I felt. I was seeking to fulfill my flesh. No tears. No emotion. But, my heart was an emotional mess. One day I asked myself, "Who am I becoming?"

Hurt, anger, rage, and a broken heart led me to being a scorned woman. In the past, I had lost control by letting other people hurt me. My mindset was no one would ever control me or abuse me again. For the first time in my life, I was wild and reckless, and my life would have been considered a reality show in the making. I laughed to hide the pain. Eventually, this revenge stricken person made me unhappy and I no longer wanted that life. The death of a friend was the catalyst that smacked me back into reality. During that time, I was in my early twenties and God snatched me from the trenches and saved me from myself. I enrolled in cosmetology school, stopped hanging out as much,

and focused on getting my life together. My time of hanging out, partying, and drinking ended abruptly, and deep down I was glad. Once I graduated from cosmetology school, I was out of the hands of one of my abusers and I felt free.

Although I had made a 180-degree turn, I was still encountering abusive relationships, but I did not revert back to getting even. Deep down I wondered what made them say they loved me, and then turn around and hit me (or cheat on me). I was tired of losing and retreated a few times. When I stopped dating in 2002, I was tired of running, screaming, defending myself, feeling depleted, being lied to, worrying, and crying. I walked away from the relationship I was in and told my daughter, "It is just me, you, and God now." I hit the floor running and served in ministry. Then the abusive and verbal attacks started again, but this time is was from (so-called) friends. People tried to degrade and belittle me. The last lost (which led me to creating the bubble and wall) took me about four years to bounce back from.

During the time I was encased within my wall and bubble, I was in a very dark place. I was hurt, angry, and confused. I knew I needed to gain control, but I did not know how. Now, when I think about it, I had reverted again. No one was going to hurt me again. I was becoming wild minded again in efforts to save myself from being hurt. The walls around me were beginning to encase me and I felt trapped. When you have been in abusive relations, you do not like to feel confined. It was to the point that

it was hard for me to accept hugs from people, including my daughter, because I felt like I was going to break. My anger had turned into rage, and I was becoming bitter instead of better.

Just stand

Oftentimes, life's obstacles can be very discouraging, heart breaking, annoying, and hard to accept or handle. That's when you take a breath, pray, and let God handle the rest. It is not that life will be all peaches and cream, but knowing when life's obstacles occur we have resiliency to withstand the whirlwind and get back up again. In the past, I would have acted a plum fool with what I have been through within the last year. I would have cursed people out, broken a few things, and gone in. Instead I took time to reflect and then I laughed. No one or nothing will ever have more control over me whereas I lose the essence of who I am or steal my joy. God has been too good to me to revert back to old mentalities.

Writing this book has been a journey and I have had various ups and downs while writing it. My main goal was to fulfill the vision God had given me, and along the way I learned a lot about business, my purpose, and myself. I never think small, especially when God gives me a vision. What God showed me was greater than I could ever imagine. When people could not see how I saw things, I had to regroup and allow God to send people who saw what I was seeing. The fear factor could not be a part of this project because it would have deterred me from completing this book and launching the women's movement.

I learned a lot during this process. I participated in webinars, watched various Facebook live videos, and joined various Facebook groups. I asked a lot of questions. But the main thing I would not do is give up. People will come and go. People will not envision things how you see them. You might lose friends along the way. In the midst of it all, do two things ... #StayFocused and #NeverGiveUp.

From the self-made bubble to FIERCE

Remember I told you that I encased myself in a self-made bubble and built a wall around my heart? I withdrew from life and did not have too much contact with people. I merely existed, but I was not living for about four years. During that time, I did a lot of reflecting, gleaning, observing, and learning. I watched relationships, friendships, and marriages. I learned about me and spent time getting to know and learn me. From it all, I was finally able to articulate what made me tick, what I wanted, and who I was. But, I had lost the power of my voice.

For about four years, I stopped serving in ministry and mentoring. Knowing that hurt people hurt people I took time to heal. There were times I would have shouting matches to release the pain and anguish. Deep down I missed the old, vibrant, witty me, but did not know how to bounce back. It seemed like every

time I bounced back something would knock me back down; kind of like a glass ceiling. The pain of my past was torturing me and I wanted to be free from the pain that was entangling me, but I did not know how. That is, until the day I cried out to God to please take away the hurt and the pain.

In January 2017, I repented to God telling Him I was sorry for running from Him for so long and surrendered my will to His will. My "yes" to walking in what He called and purposed me to do opened so many doors for me. It has been a journey, but I thank God for never leaving me nor forsaking me while I endured the tests and trials of life. Although I have been through the fire, I do not smell like smoke or brimstone. Now, I have been empowered to walk in my purpose and my comeback game is stronger than ever. I thank God for positioning and pruning me so I can be a blessing to others. My main goal was to become better; not bitter. I know I had to deal with my hurt instead of ignoring it. I finally let the healing process begin and it felt great.

In a state of awe – a poem
EVER…?

Ever needed to express yourself, but could not find the words to say and did not know why

The words never seemed to express your feelings no matter how much you tried

Ever needed to tell someone the things you were going through

And to your surprise there was no one there to listen to you

Ever been shut up and pushed away so much that a pen and paper became your best friends

Although they could not supply any answers, at least you could get a word in

Ever found that you had out-grown the friends you used to hang around

The more you talked to them the lower they brought you down

Ever encountered an experience that was too shameful to tell

If others knew what you had done, they would hope you'd rot in hell

Ever felt like no one really cares about what you say or what you do

So you hide yourself from the world and wonder how you will make it through

Ever had a memory that haunts you so much you cannot sleep

Something so painful and disturbing that you lose your desire to eat

So much pain occurring at one time that you wonder who could possibly see you through

You realize that only God can help you for there is nothing He cannot do

Ever found yourself wanting to say something that was on your mind

Then you realize it hurts too much and the wound had not been healed by time

Ever been in a relationship that was not making you happy and did not feel right

But every time you tried to leave you knew there would be a fight

Ever found yourself wanting to grow and seek a higher level

And with this new desire for growth, you faced all kinds of temptation from the devil

Ever felt like an outcast and a stranger in your own home

So you go into prayer, you cast out demons and now you no longer feel alone

Ever felt like you were not cute and no one really cared about you or how you felt

So you go along with the game and find out the cards had already been dealt

So much pain, so much to endure, you feel you can't handle it and look to the heavens above

That's when God picks you up and embraces you with His unconditional love

Ever thought you could not go on and tried to end it all

Then you hear a Voice and notice that your name is the one the Voice calls

It tells you to stay encouraged, do not give up - for God will see you through

To just hold on and to keep the faith for He is not through blessing you

Now whenever I feel alone, I thank God for speaking to me and helping me through

My faith has grown, I have new friends and the life He has

given me is brand new

I used to worry whether or not I was loved or liked or if I had true friends

God answered all my prayers and I can honestly say I've been born again

Thank You Lord for opening my blinded eye to see

That what You have for me, it is for me!

• **Kimberly, 08/27/99©** •

How to no longer host pity parties, but instead recover and become resilient

Pity parties are the 'oh woe is me' parties that drain you and your friends. In order to no longer host pity parties, but instead recover and become resilient, you have to be willing to listen to reason. Your true friends offer wise counsel and help you bounce back. They offer tissue and hugs for a moment, but will not allow you wallow in self-pity. True friends do not say I do not know what is wrong with her, but instead hold your arms up when you are weak. In your difficult seasons, you learn who your true friends are.

The time has come to shake yourself loose from the drama and position yourself to go after your purpose. No longer shall you host or attend pity parties, but instead prepare and plan for your next. Everything happens for a reason. Determine what the lesson is, document it, learn from it, and move on. Then it is time to put on your big girl panties, weather the storm, pray, and

come back stronger than before.

Rubber band tenacity

According to Google Dictionary, tenacity is defined as "the quality or fact of being very determined; the quality or fact of continuing to exist; determination; persistence." A rubber band is a piece of stretchy material that is used to hold things together. When a rubber band is stretched, it bounces back to its original shape and form (unless it is broken, but stay focused I am going somewhere).

Having rubber band tenacity means when you are stretched or tested, your come back game is strong due to your determination and persistence to be victorious even when things do not seem that way. Being resilient is having rubber band tenacity. Living a F.I.E.R.C.E. lifestyle is having rubber band tenacity because you are persistent and determined to bounce back from the instances that tried to destroy you. Yes, what made me love me was making my come back game strong, no longer wallowing in the pain from my past, and being persistent and determined to succeed.

Tests and trials come to make us strong. I know that seems strange or like a cliché, but it is true. Think about it this way – when something is tested, it goes through a series of events or occurrences to prove how strong or durable it is. Cars go through a series of tests for highway safety and crash testing. These series

of tests allow car manufacturers to find out what is not operating correctly to build a stronger, safer car. Gold goes through a refining process to remove impurities and other ingredients are added to make it stronger. Earlier in this chapter, we mentioned 1 Peter 5:10 – "But the God of grace, after you have suffered a while, make you perfect, stablish, strengthen, settle you." After you have been processed, tested, and refined, God will strengthen you. It might not feel like it while you are going through, but God is not a man that He would lie, and His word tells us He will never leave us nor forsake us. #TrustGod #Believe

Daily affirmations

Your list of daily affirmations is expanding. Here is a new list. Recite for the next three days.

I am beautiful.
I am successful.
I am smart.
I am a lender and not a borrower.
I am above and not beneath.
I am wealthy.
I am on the road to discovering my identity and love for self.
I love me.
I am not the lies that have been spoken over me.
I will not believe the lies others have said to me.
I will no longer walk in fear.

I am not a failure.
I am creative.
I am renewing my mind.
I am victorious.
I am able to recover from difficult situations.
I, (your name), am a success story – not a tragedy.
I am Fearless.
I am Innovative.
I am Empowered.
I am Resilient.

Reflection

How did you feel stating the affirmations? Was it hard looking

at yourself in the mirror? Were you being truthful and transparent? Journal and reflect on the experience here.

_____
_____
_____
_____
_____
_____
_____
_____
_____
_____
_____
_____
_____
_____

LIFE APPLICATION:

What are you going to do to break through your glass ceiling to become resilient?

In this section, journal what you will do to become resilient.

It is time to put what we have discussed and what you journaled into action. This will become your action plan as you prepare and apply what you have learned to receive your break through.

_____

_____

_____

_____

_____

_____

_____

_____

_____

_____

Resilient Prayer

Oh, Holy One, I come to You this day giving You all the glory and the honor, lifting You up my King, my Lord, My

God. I give You praise for helping me walk in Your word so that I may be strengthened. I give You praise for keeping my mind strengthened. I give You praise for You have made me courageous and I am not afraid or discouraged. I give You praise for You, Lord God, are with me wherever I go. I am covered and protected under your right hand of power and authority and I am resilient. I am under Your shadow and nothing shall by any means harm me for You made me resilient. I am resting in Your cleft and You lift my arms up daily. With Your strength, and I can run through a troop and leap over a wall. I thank You that there is nothing that I cannot do because You are with me daily. Thank You for having Your angels encamped around me and for keeping me safe. Amen

CONFIDENT

What does confident mean?

The fifth strategy of the journey to live a F.I.E.R.C.E. lifestyle is to become confident in who you are. You develop confidence by knowing your worth. According to Google Dictionary, confident is defined as "feeling or showing confidence in oneself; self-assured." The most difficult place to be is at a point in which you do not believe in yourself. Confidence can be hard to display at times, but once we overcome fear, know who we are, become empowered, and strengthen our comeback game, we are able to exert a greater level of confidence.

Confident versus Arrogant

While confident is defined as self-assurance, according to Google Dictionary, arrogance is defined as "having or revealing an exaggerated sense of one's own importance or abilities." With arrogance, the person is as the youth say, "doing too much or being extra." It is great to have balance whereas our confidence does not turn into arrogance where we think no one is better than us. No matter what, remain humble.

> *"But he giveth more grace. Wherefore he saith, God resisteth the proud, but giveth grace unto the humble"*
>
> • James 4:6, King James Version •

People will not be able to handle the new and improved you, and that is okay. Do not retreat or give up. Stay focused. Just know that misery loves company and stop entertaining anything that does not build you up. Focus on no longer being miserable.

Life is full of surprises, ups, downs, triumphs, let downs, victories, setbacks, and fun. The peaks and valleys are what make us stronger, more confident, and resilient. Focusing on the negative aspects of life is no longer an option. The important thing is to do what will tip the scale in your favor. Let's build up our confidence so that we are self-assured in what God has positioned us to do.

Hey you, your confidence is showing! Hold your head up and look the world in the face. My father used to tell me, "Do not walk with your head down. Look the world in the face. Observe your surroundings, and do not be afraid to look someone in the eyes when you are talking to them. When you are afraid to look people in the eyes, you appear timid. Good eye contact displays confidence." His words boosted my self-esteem, gave me confidence of understanding my self-worth, and showed me how to present myself to others. Always remember – body language often speaks louder than words.

Somehow the years of isolation made me lose the importance of eye contact, because back then I never wanted anyone to look me in my years. But, each day I am getting better at exerting good eye contact.

Life story
Lack of love shielded me from believing in myself

Since certain family members did not display love towards

me, their lack of concern and love kept me from believing in myself. I did not know who I was. For years, I walked around with a piece of my identity missing. All I knew was how to survive and never give up, but I was not confident in who I was and did not think I had anything to offer anyone. Over the years, people have taken advantage of me due to my kind heart and generous Spirit. The years of manipulation and abuse led to mistrust and anger.

Many people look at the relationship I have with my daughter and consider me to be a good mother. Well, I beg to differ. I consider her to be a great daughter because she is willing to listen. My father used to talk to me a lot and tell me about life. When I became a parent, all I knew was to talk about life and tell the truth. I have made numerous mistakes raising her, but I am always humble enough to admit my mistakes, apologize, and find different ways to teach her about life.

Suffering from low self-esteem

I suffered from low self-esteem for years. One day my father showed me a Sister Sledge album cover. Sister Sledge was a popular singing group comprised of four African American sisters known for the song, We are Family. My father said, "What do you see when you look at them?" I stared long and hard at the album cover and responded, "Me."

On this particular album cover, the members of Sister Sledge

had their hair pulled back in a ponytail and very little make-up on. The album cover displayed the true essence of their beauty. I always thought I had a large forehead and nose. When I saw them showing their forehead, I became confident with showing mine as well. My father's purpose for showing me the album cover was to boost my self-esteem. I was concerned with different aspects of my looks and not looking a certain way made me sad.

After my father's self-esteem talk, I started to feel better about myself and realized my own unique beauty. My nose told its own story as well as my other features that I did not like. Instead of not liking who I saw in the mirror, I chose to adore her and accept her how she was created to be.

> *"I will praise thee; for I am fearfully and wonderfully made: marvellous are thy works; and that my soul knoweth right well"*
>
> • Psalm 139:14, King James Version •

Ahhhh, this Scripture helped me understand who I was and who I was destined to be. How could I hate God's creation? A new outlook on life and a new perspective helped me learn my worth and become more confident with who I was. Now, do you see why a renewed mind is important?

The Woman in the Mirror

My face tells a story of my life. In fourth grade, I burned 75% of my cornea due to hot chili splashing in my right eye. The

doctor told my parents I might be blind in that eye. Three days later, that same doctor said, "It's a miracle", when he removed the bandages from my eye, examined my eye, and realized I had 20/20 vision. In fifth grade, I injured my nose when I tripped on a step. At the age of 18, I was in a car accident and my nose was broken from hitting the dashboard. My eyes are small, but my vision has always been keen, and at a young age I could see things prophetically. I had to learn to love the woman in the mirror – flaws and all. So many people hated and despised me that it made me belittle and hate myself. The time had finally come to flip the script and learn to love the woman in the mirror, but how?

I think I am finally getting a grasp on life and my quest for love. Am I perfect? Of course not. Do I have all of the answers? Not this girl. But I can say this… I am learning all that I can in this season to be all God has called me to be forever. The time has come for me to walk away from what I have known life to be and begin to embrace the newness surrounding me. You see, no longer does my past dictate my future, but instead, I set the course for where my life is heading. Greatness is coming. It is harvest time for all the years I have sown in tears. It was not until I discovered who I was and understood my worth that I broke free from my past. No longer will pain and heartache entangle me. Those days are dead and gone.

Lessons I taught my daughter to build her confidence

My daughter is five feet tall. She used to be very sad about her height. One day I told her, "Unfortunately, there is nothing you can really do about your height so you should not allow that to make you sad." Years later, my daughter later told me how my words made her feel better because she realized there was nothing she could do about her height so she began to focus on her strengths instead of being infatuated about her height. This made my heart glad.

Oftentimes, we let other people's opinions of us determine how we feel about our self or how we view our self. I knew how that felt, and I did not want her to go through life torturing herself about something she had no real control over as well as other people's negative thoughts of her. Never allow someone's negative opinion of you become your opinion of yourself.

I never wanted my daughter to feel like she was alienated or did not belong somewhere. At a young age, I took her to what is considered one of the most expensive shopping areas and let her know she belonged there because her money had the same purchasing power as everyone else's money. I wanted this experience to help her understand her worth and have a positive stance in life.

Reclaiming our identity

Since the Biblical days when the people asked God for a king, we have been doomed to a life of appeasing man. God warned us,

but we wanted someone to see and who could have rule over us (read 1 Samuel 8). Somewhere along the way we lost the essence of our purpose and our vision became distorted. We focus more on pleasing others than pleasing God. The time has come for us to reclaim our identity in order to walk in our purpose.

How do we reclaim your identity? How do we find the pieces that were lost? How do we restore what was broken? Honestly, it is all a process.

To reclaim your identity, you have to figure out what is missing from your life so you can find the pieces that were lost. This will eventually bring resolution to restore what was broken.

For me, my missing identity was in the fact that my family members did not love me. Did love make him hang me from the fourth floor window? Did love have them play catch with me, as if I were a ball, and one of them move? Did love compare me to others and belittle me? Did love lead me to hiding in my closet wishing someone would find me or notice I was missing? Did love make me want something to happen to me (nothing major) so I could feel like someone cared? This lack of love made me question my identity in the sense of not feeling worthy to be loved. Since my own family did not love me, I felt no one loved me, and it was hard for me to receive true, genuine love from others.

After a while, I began to seek what was lost. I looked for

someone to love me, but even in that they could not fill the void I was experiencing. My heart was broken and this love quest tormented me mentally. I decided to reevaluate my life. From my life evaluation, I learned my identity could not be found in the eyes, arms, or voice of someone else, but instead it had to come from within me and understand God's love for me. But before I could understand God's love for me, I needed to learn how to love myself.

As I began to build my self-confidence by restoring the brokenness of the woman in the mirror, I began to feel hope and love. No longer was my pain driven on the lack of love from my family members. Instead, I began to rejoice in the fact that I loved myself. I could finally look at my reflection and smile at who I saw, and not cry. What was lost was actually lying dormant inside of me. Reading God's Word helped me restore the broken areas. The process went on for years, but then God gave me the final piece to the puzzle for my life. The final piece of the puzzle was the word F.I.E.R.C.E. followed by giving me what the acronym stood for:

Fearless • Innovative • Empowered • Resilient • Confident • Exuberant

After God spoke this word to me, He showed me how He made me F.I.E.R.C.E.

Please visit my website **www.FierceWomenEmp.com**
for information on e-courses and workshops to live a F.I.E.R.C.E. lifestyle.

Slowly restoring my confidence – a poem
The Cry

If I told you everything I wanted to say, could you handle it? If I told you of my pain and anguish as a child, would you care? If I told you about the times I wanted to end it all, would you laugh? If I told you about the tears I've cried, would you hug me? Lied on, cheated on, and hit on for no reason. There was a point in my life that the devil had me believing there was something wrong with me. He had me in a state of low self-esteem. I didn't care if anyone liked me, because my own family didn't like me. It was to a point that I didn't even like myself.

I believe each tear I cried, God shed one too. At times, I felt like such a failure. Each time I tried to get things right, something would happen and I ended up taking two steps backwards. Big dreams. High aspirations. How do I bring them to fruition? I'm not cute enough or talented enough to be recognized by such a materialistic world. What do I do? Where do I turn? Who will hear my cry? Who will help me now?

It took years of prayer, belief, and faith to finally get to a point of understanding God had a purpose for me, and that I was destined for greatness. For years I held onto years of pain, anguish, and disappointment. If I didn't expect much, then I didn't have to worry about much. The devil is a liar!

Some of my friends envied me and looked up to me, but I never understood why. I was a child of divorced parents. My parents worked hard each day to make ends meet. I loved my family dearly, but never the same amount of love I gave out, but I still loved them anyway. As my teenage years approached, I looked for love in all the wrong places.

My life consisted of hanging out, drinking, and working. Abusive relationships made me doubt myself and often had me running for my life, people hiding me, and pulling out knives for protection to stop my abusers. After being elected president of my community college program, I asked the preceding president what they saw in me that made them vote for me. He told me, "They voted for you because they see something in you what you do not see in yourself."

Suddenly, this life was boring and after an encounter with God at a funeral, I enrolled in school. I completed cosmetology school, and then enrolled in a community college. My goal was to be a desairologist. I was starting to feel good about myself. It had taken some time, but I was getting back on track. I started attending church. Then the devil set another trap. The choices I was making were destroying me. Feeling sorry for people, and getting into relationships I knew I should not have been in. Once I even had a guy determining my destiny in a speeding car to kill both us or at least himself. God really loves me, because I'm still here despite the foolish choices I have made in life. Always trying to be the peacemaker and the one to hold everything together, and always the one getting hurt. Always the one being stepped on, lied on, cheated on, hit on, used, abused, scorned, and spit on. Who deserves such treatment and torture? Not to mention the uncle who tried to molest me, or the male best friends who tried to use me. Thank You, God, for grace and mercy! Many of nights I've cried out, 'Lord, why me?!' Thank You, God for restoring me and building my confidence to endure and stand strong.

• **Kimberly, 12/02/2004©** •

How to develop self-assurance so you can become more

confident in who you are and understand your self-worth

Look in the mirror. What do you see? Write what you see below…

_____
_____
_____
_____
_____
_____
_____
_____
_____
_____
_____
_____
_____
_____

Now, I am going to ask a question. Did you list negative aspects

or characteristics about yourself? Back in the day, my list would have read – "my forehead is big, my body finally grew to accommodate my large head, my eyes are small, and my nose is big." I would have listed everything that tainted my confidence.

Today, my list would read, "I see a woman who has endured a lot of pain, but she has the courage to withstand all of the haters and naysayers. I see a woman who wants the best for others more than she wants the best for herself. I see a woman who is self-less, caring, and loving. I see scars that tell a story and eyes that are fixed on impacting the world." The difference in my lists is due to a renewed mind and my determination of living a F.I.E.R.C.E. lifestyle. When I look at me, I see my potential instead of my pain, and I see my future instead of my past. Seeing myself differently is due to having confidence in myself and a renewed mind.

Now, look in the mirror again and tell me what you see. I want you to know and understand your worth. Speak life into yourself. Speak to the woman you are becoming. Speak to the woman you were destined to be. Write what you see below…

_____
_____
_____
_____
_____
_____
_____
_____
_____
_____
_____
_____
_____
_____
_____
_____

YOU NO LONGER HAVE PERMISSION TO DOWNGRADE YOURSELF.
Remember the poem, *Our Deepest Fear?*

"Who am I to be brilliant, gorgeous, talented, fabulous? Actually, who are you not to be? You are a child of God. Your playing small does not serve the world. There is nothing enlightened about shrinking so that other people won't feel insecure around you."

You have the right to be beautiful, gorgeous, confident, talented you! No longer will you minimize your abilities and talents to pacify someone else. No longer will you feel inadequate because of low self-esteem. God created you in His image. You are powerful, you are creative, you are wonderful, and you shall walk in boldness and confidence of who God created and purposed you to be. The world needs your inventions, books, designs, and creativity. You have been positioned for purpose and God is doing a new thing in you. I am so glad we are taking this journey together to get you to the place God has ordained for you since you were in your mother's womb. I am so excited about your future and how you are about to collide with your purpose! Yes, what made me love me was the day I could look myself in the mirror with loving eyes and walk in confidence knowing God destined me for purpose and greatness.

How does Confidence Portray Itself

Confidence is about knowing your self-worth. It is knowing what you will and will not tolerate. It is about walking in your purpose. It is being self-empowered and loving yourself. It is knowing your likes and dislikes. It is knowing what makes you tick. It is being able to effectively communicate who you are. It is about having charisma whereas you attract people who are called to be a part of your purpose. It is never cocky, prideful, proud, or rude. Confidence is having a fierceness about you and knowing how to go after what is yours. A tiger does not glance its eyes on prey that it does not think it can capture. A tiger fixes is eyes on what it wants and has the confidence to capture it. Confidence is having the eye of the tiger and a tiger's pounce.

Be Strong and Confident in Who You Are

When I was little, females did not like me when I stepped on the scene. They would try to fight me or try to pull my hair. Several times people have told me that others see something in me that I did not see in myself. I get it now…my confidence was showing. Some people loved it; while others wanted to destroy it. There was never a point in my life where I was cocky or arrogant because my father did not allow that, but being confident in myself was always what he attempted to instill in me.

When you hold your head whereas you look the world in the face and you know your purpose as well as who you are, there will be

haters and naysayers who will attempt to destroy you or call you prideful. No, you are not cocky, arrogant, or prideful – you are confident in who God has called you to be. You are confident in walking in your purpose. You are confident in being all God called you to be. Remember what we learned before … no more playing small or feeling less than. God has positioned you for greatness and He needs you so you can bless others and snatch them from the things that are keeping them bound.

When you walk in confidence, your stride is different. Your mentality is different. Your mind is renewed and your perception in keen. Be you. Do you. Be strong and courageous. Never become "all that" whereas you lose focus and become proud, cocky, and/or arrogant. Be confident and humble. When you become confident, you become unstoppable.

> *"Likewise, ye younger, submit yourselves unto the elder. Yea, all of you be subject one to another, and be clothed with humility: for God resisteth the proud, and giveth grace to the humble"*
> • 1 Peter 5:5, King James Version •

When you are F.IE.R.C.E., it is important to know who you are. The world judges you based on their opinion of you, but it is very important that you do not allow other people's negative opinion of you to become your opinion of yourself. It is important to analyze yourself, map out a plan for your life, and find the tools you need to fulfill the plan for your life.

"For I know the thoughts that I think toward you. saith the Lord, thoughts of peace and not of evil, to give you an expected end"

• Jeremiah 29:11, King James Version •

God has a plan for our life. Many times we drift away from the plan and even take a different route. Eventually, we realize what has occurred has set us off course, and then we begin to realign ourselves according to what has been destined and purposed for us.

"For whatsoever is born of God overcometh the world and this is the victory that overcometh the world, even our faith"

(1 John 5:4, King James Version).

"Being confident of this very thing, that he which hath begun a good work in you will perform it until the day of Jesus Christ:"

(Philippians 1:6).

Daily affirmations

Your list of daily affirmations is expanding. Here is a new list to recite for the next three days.

I am beautiful.
I am successful.
I am smart.
I am a lender and not a borrower.
I am above and not beneath.
I am wealthy.
I am on the road to discovering my identity and love for self.
I love me.
I am not the lies that have been spoken over me.
I will not believe the lies others have said to me.
I will no longer walk in fear.
I am not a failure.
I am creative.
I am renewing my mind.
I am victorious.
I am able to recover from difficult situations.
I walk in confidence.
I know who I am.
I am refined.
I am valuable.
I know my worth.
I, (your name), am a success story – not a tragedy.
I am Fearless.
I am Innovative.
I am Empowered.
I am Resilient.
I am Confident.

Reflection

How did you feel stating the affirmations? Was it hard looking at yourself in the mirror? Were you being truthful and transparent? Journal and reflect on the experience here…

_____

_____

_____

_____

_____

_____

_____

_____

_____

_____

_____

_____

_____

LIFE APPLICATION:
What are you going to do to break through your glass ceiling to understand your self-worth and become confident in who God created you to be?

In this section, journal what you will do to walk in confidence.

It is time to put what we have discussed and what you journaled into action. This will become your action plan as you prepare and apply what you have learned to receive your break through.

_____

_____

_____

_____

_____

_____

_____

_____

_____

_____

Confident Prayer

Father I come to You this day trusting You and believing You for all things that You have concerning me. I know, Lord, that You have plans to prosper me and not to harm me; plans to give me hope and a future. Father, I have faith in all that concerns my purpose and destiny. I have faith to believe that greater is coming. Oh Lord, You have set my paths straight, You have healed me, You have delivered me, and my time of prosperity is coming forth quickly. Father, I thank You that You are moving me from the back to the front quickly. I thank You that what You have for me is generational and flowing through my blood line. Oh my sustainer, El Shaddai, I thank You that You are with me even today. Father, I thank You and bless Your Holy name that You have given me another push to go further. Amen

EXUBERANT

What does exuberant mean?

The sixth strategy of the journey to live a F.I.E.R.C.E. lifestyle is to become exuberant about life. According to Google Dictionary, exuberant is defined as "filled with or characterized by a lively energy and excitement." Exerting lively energy and excitement makes you appreciate and embrace life in a new way. It helps you value life and place things into perspective. It also helps you love you and know your worth. When you are exuberant, you live your life like it is golden, embrace your potential and purpose, and live life to the fullest extent.

> *"It's ok if you fall down and lose your spark. Just make sure that when you get back up, you rise as the whole damn fire."*
> • **Colette Werden** •

This quote by Colette Werden is my new motto when life gets overwhelming or I feel like I have lost my focus. For a long time, I did not allow myself to be human. I was my worst critic and if things did not go right I would beat myself up about it. Now, I understand failing is a part of learning and growing. Renewing my mind and having a resilient attitude towards life have allowed my come back game to be strengthened. When life hits me, I come back stronger and more intense than before, and learn

from what occurred. Things may happen, but through it all I am determined to never give up. If you lose focus and your spark becomes weak, when you resurface, rise up as the whole damn fire whereas you are stronger and more intense than before.

What lights your fire and excites you?

What is it that lights your fire and excites you in a way that makes you want to strive for better? What is it that you enjoy doing? What makes you smile? For me, it is empowering others. See, I know what it is like to walk around sad and depressed. I love seeing people smile and helping them reach their next level in life. Honestly, that sparks me and pushes me to do more. When I see someone with low self-esteem, before I leave their presence, I tell them we need to stay connected and hand them my business card. My goal is to impact others' lives by imparting the importance of self-empowerment and self-love.

Write what pushes and drives you below...

_____

_____

_____

_____

_____

_____

_____

_____

_____

Purpose

I know some of you had to ponder on what sparks you and that is okay as long as you came up with a truthful answer. Actually, what you have written is tied to your purpose. Let's revisit a familiar Scripture.

> *"For I know the thoughts that I think toward you, saith the Lord, thoughts of peace, and not of evil, to give you an expected end"*
> • Jeremiah 29:11, King James Version •

God has a plan and purpose for our life. We dishonor God when we do not realize what our purpose is. Remember we talked about utilizing our talents and writing the things we enjoy doing which showed our creativity? Now, we need to walk in what God has purposed us to do. Don't you dare quit now! We rid ourselves of stinking thinking (negative thoughts) chapters ago.

People often say, "Well, you have it together. You know what your purpose is. I just cannot figure out what I am supposed to do." That's just it. You are trying to figure it out and God has already told you what to do because He placed it in you a long time ago. You just are not seeing it as your purpose. Walking in your purpose does not always call you to a platform. It is operating in the gifts that God has placed within you.

I want you to read 1 Corinthians 12 – the entire chapter so you understand spiritual gifts. Then, I want you to ponder on what you like doing that fulfills you and blesses others, which is your gift (talent). Write your gifts below…

_____
_____
_____
_____
_____
_____
_____
_____
_____
_____
_____
_____
_____
_____
_____

Pessimist versus Optimist: What is your Perspective of Life?

Is your glass half empty or half full? Pessimists say, "My glass is half empty." Optimists say, "My glass is half full." Pessimists are negative and expect the worst. Optimists are upbeat and look at the bright side of things. Your perspective says a lot about your energy and your drive. Are you drinking from a half empty or half full glass? Are you viewing life your through the front window or the rear view mirror? Are you walking around with blinders on?

It is amazing how once the blinders are removed from our eyes how clearly we can see. Blinders are put on horses to keep them focused so the things around them do not distract them. When horses have on blinders, they can only see what is straight ahead and they have one view of things. Well, for humans, blinders provide a limited view and can prevent someone from operating in their full potential. According to Google Dictionary, binders are defined as "something that prevents someone from gaining a full understanding of a situation." God has so much in store for us, but it is time to think outside of the box, stop limiting our view, and change our perspective of things. It is time to take off our blinders and view life from all angles.

#PutItAllInPerspective   #ChangeYourPerception
#NoTunnelVision   #ExploreAndSoar
#BeFIERCE

Jack in the Box Mentality

Picture a jack in the box toy. There is a box with a handle on it. As the handle on the box is turned, music plays. Expect the unexpected because at any moment something will pop out of the box. When the toy pops out of the box, the person holding the box usually jumps and laughs. Then, the person pushes the toy back into the box and does the process all over again.

Are you living your life like a jack in the box toy? Are you living your life in spurts whereas you are good once you are free from certain things? Do you feel free until something occurs and you are stuffed back into a box where you are comfortable, context, and confined? It is time to live outside of the box and break free from the jack in the box mentality.

Now, I am giving you permission to break from the jack in the box mentality and shine bright like a diamond. I am turning the handle on the jack in the box of your life and once you pop up I am going to cut you loose and break the handle. NO ONE (not even you) will stuff you in the box again! Today is the day you break free from the jack in the box mentality of conforming to the ways of the world.

> *"And be not conformed to this world: but be ye transformed by the renewing of your mind, that ye may prove what is that good, and acceptable, and perfect, will of God"*
>
> • Romans 12:2, King James Version •

From this day forth, you will live an exuberant, energized, free life. Nothing and no one (not even you) will confine you again. It is time to live.

"The thief cometh not, but for to steal, and to kill, and to destroy: I am come that they might have life, and that they might have it more abundantly"
• John 10:10, King James Version •

It is time to live the life Christ died for you to have. It is time to live an abundant life. It is time to be free from negative thoughts, feeling inferior, and not operating at your full potential. No more small thinking. It is time to live!

Life story
The Decision to Carry On My Father's Legacy

Why would I smile when my heart was in so many fragmented pieces? My heart had been re-glued so many times nothing was strong enough to hold it together or fix it was my thought process. That is until God gave me so many reasons to smile, trust, heal, and love again.

Death can teach you so much about life and setting priorities. When my father passed away in 2010, I lost a part of my spark. I put off grieving for two years. My daughter's friend was killed in 2012 and while at a counseling session for the youth, a counselor asked how I was doing. I started to say, "Okay", but a part of

me started talking and crying out. The counselor began to give me advice. I told her I had not cried or allowed myself to grieve because it was not going to bring my father back. She reassured me that I needed to let out my emotions and it was okay to cry. A few days later, I went to see my Spiritual mom and she told me that there are five stages of bereavement (denial, anger, bargaining, depression, and acceptance) and if you do not go through each stage, you will get stuck. I was stuck because I kept repeating certain stages. I had moved from denial and was stuck in anger and bargaining. Learning this gave me the strength to go through all of the stages and allow myself to grieve.

As a part of my grieving and healing process, I drove past the last places my father and I had lived and called his best friend whom I had not talked to in two years. Talking to his best friend made me feel a lot better. He had lost my number and had been trying to reach me. When I returned home, I pulled out my father's ashes and began to talk and apologize to him. I apologized for being angry with him for leaving me. He had a stroke in 2009 and passed away 14 months later. I needed my best friend. He was my superman. There was so much we were supposed to do in life, but he was gone. In my mind, I knew he was in a lot of pain and I did not like seeing him in pain. My heart still wanted him here and it was broken from the void of no longer having him in my life. This was a day of comfort and release and I began to feel a peace come over me. I cried, I screamed, and I exhaled.

Five years after my father's death, I began slipping into depression and was on the verge of a nervous breakdown. I could not concentrate on anything. I was in school earning my Master's degree and could barely keep up with my assignments. My mind was wandering all over the place, and I had to play all of this off when my daughter was around. One day I cried out, "Lord, this pain is too much. I cannot take it anymore." Instantly, God gave me a peace that I had not felt in years.

See, I was afraid of totally healing because I did not want to let my father go. I had to learn and understand I was not letting him go, but instead needed to fulfill his legacy. When I began to view things in regards to fulfilling my father's legacy, I became driven to live life with purpose and change the status quo of my life. No longer would I settle on being mediocre, but instead, wanted to live life abundantly.

> *"Now unto him that is able to do exceeding abundantly above all that we ask or think, according to the power that worketh in us"*
>
> • Ephesians 3:20, King James Version •

CPR – Changed my Perspective and Reality

I came out of my funk a little bit, but I was still hurting from the pain of other life occurrences. When I stopped running from God and yielded my will to His, things began to change and doors began to open, but I was still hurting. When my godmother

passed in May 2017, I thought about how sometimes it was difficult for her to breathe. This lit a spark within me to actually live instead of merely existing. Since my godmother often fought to breathe, I became determined to no longer take breathing or life for granted. It was as if God resuscitated and jumpstarted my drive and passion for life. The pain from my past was no longer tormenting me. I found new reasons to live. I stopped letting other things control me and began to control the situation as well as the outcome. For years, I was questioning what happened that destroyed so much of my life around me, but on this day, God gave me peace and renewed strength. God freed my mind from the thoughts that were tormenting me and sparked a new drive in me. I decided to let go of my pain and live life.

Once again, I was excited about life and making a difference in others' lives.

> *"Therefore if any man be in Christ, he is a new creature: old things are passed away; behold, all things are become new"*
> • 2 Corinthians 5:17, King James Version •

I had my spark back and I stopped running from my purpose. I began to put things in motion. Early in 2017, God said, "Reconciliation." I was seeing reconciliation all around me with friendships. I was in awe of how God was changing things around me. Thank You, Lord, for performing CPR on me by changing my perspective and reality.

The birth of the F.I.E.R.C.E. Movement

One day my godfather said, "You have a tiger's pounce. I like that about you. You do not let people treat you any kind of way and you know how to speak up for yourself." His words stuck with me. A few days later, I heard the Lord say, "FIERCE." I inquired more from the Lord and He said, "FIERCE Women's Empowerment Movement. This will not be local, but instead it will be international." God began to send people my way to help me stay focused and bring His vision to fruition. Not only was my spark back, but I had come back as the whole fire.

God placed people around me who believed in me, pushed me, supported me, inspired me, and stood by me through so much. I thank God for placing them in my life. Suddenly, my spark was back and my smile returned as well. I realized the process God had been taking me through and I was ready to take the world by storm.

With anything that is birthed, there are labor pains. My smile was tested, finances to complete the book were depleted before finishing it, and health concerns arose, but my faith was stronger than ever and I did not waver. Being resilient made me withstand the tests and come through the fire without smelling like brimstone. Had I not become F.I.E.R.C.E, I probably would have gone back into my self-made bubble.

"Being confident of this very thing, that he which hath begun a good work in you will perform it until the day of Jesus Christ"

• Philippians 1:6, King James Version •

The Importance of Going through Each Stage of the Process

With healing and restoration, there are stages we must go through. As with learning about the five stages of bereavement when my father died and the importance of going through each stage of bereavement so I would not remain stuck in a stage, the same thing applies with other aspects of life. If it is a death, lost job, relationship break-up, friendship break-down, or divorce, there are stages you need to go through for your resiliency, come back game, healing, and restoration.

As with this book, you have to go in order and complete each strategy for a complete understanding of F.I.E.R.C.E. and to become self-empowered and develop a love for self. Do not force yourself through the process or stage of recovery, but also do not stay complacent and stuck. Obtain a healthy balance. It is important to research information regarding what you are going through and feeling. Connect with people who will pour into you. Take time to heal. Be honest with yourself. Allow yourself to be hurt and cry. Then, reignite your spark and come back more intense than before and as the whole fire. Let the quote by Colette Warden motivate you.

There is a reason God called this a Movement

Movement is not something that is complacent or stands still. Movement is always going, always evolving, and always changing. According to Google Dictionary, movement is defined as "(1) an act of changing physical location or position or of having this changed; (2) a group of people working together to advance their shared political, social, or artistic ideas." F.I.E.R.C.E. Women's Empowerment Movement is a catalyst to ignite women's spark for life and empower them to come back from life's tests and trials as the whole fire.

How I Regained My Smile and Spark

Each day is full of new mercies, but it is also full of occurrences that can make us happy or sad. I regained my smile and spark by no longer being afraid of what the day had in store for me, but instead, greeting each day head on and riding the wave. Instances in life are going to occur no matter what and are out of my control, but how I react to these instances is the only thing I have control over. Once I changed my perspective about life, I vowed to give whatever I was doing my all. I changed my wardrobe to display confidence and fierceness, and incorporated a 'slay daily' mentality. On days I was not feeling my best, I allowed myself to be human, but made sure I still exerted a positive attitude. Changing my perspective and outlook on life gave me the ability to smile again and reignited my spark.

When Will I See You Smile Again

When I gave up on me, God positioned people in my life to relight my spark and make me smile. Smiling now feels natural and it feels great. Some of the things that had been taken away have been restored as God saw fit. Never allow anything or anyone to have so much control over you that it permanently takes away your smile and your joy. Also, understand some losses are not as detrimental as we think, but are actually for our good. Have you encountered a friendship or relationship in which you were no longer on the same level? If you had stayed, it would have delayed or deleted your ability to see your self-worth and walk in your purpose. Now that God has conducted CPR on you by Changing your Perspective and Reality, you are able to walk in your purpose. Get ready because the best is yet to come.

Guess what? I have been positioned in your life to restore your smile and spark. You are not alone during this process! I am here with you every step of the way. Know that the choice is yours. Failure is not an option. Giving up is not an option. #LetsDoThis

**Visit my website
www.FierceWomenEmp.com
for coaching opportunities to work together on this process.**

The path to finding myself – a poem

Finally

I never thought I'd tell this story.
Never thought the words would ever flow correctly.
Never thought this day would come.
Is this a dream come true?
Could this really be?
My heart has been hurting so much lately.
I played the fool so many times.
Once again, my heart is hurting.
Once again, there is pain to bear.
No one really loves me.
No one really appreciates me.
People think that I am a jealous hearted person.
Some people think I am crazy.
Once upon a time, I thought the same thing.
But right now I feel so used.
Right now I feel alone.
Right now I feel abandoned.
Right now I feel drained.
Gave too much.
Gave my life, my heart, my peace.
How do I regain it all?
Do I really want to?
Always sitting in a state of wonder and thought.
A certain person told me that he would never hurt me.

He lied and he said he would not lie to me.

He said he would not leave me.

He is gone just like the others.

Took the goods and ran along about his way.

Once again, I sit with eyes full of tears.

Lord, what is wrong?

Is there something wrong me with me?

What could I have done to deserve this?

Someone please tell me what I should do?

I give my heart too easily.

This time I will lock my heart and throw away the key.

This time I am throwing in my cards.

And never again will the Queen of Hearts be dealt.

Have you ever done something that hurt so many people and that hurt you so much?

Lord, please help me take the pain away!

I have been hit for the last time.

I have felt this lonely feeling for the last time.

I have cried for the last time.

Finally, I have the strength to regain what was lost.

Finally, I am back in control!

Glory to God!

• **Kimberly, 05/09/01©** •

Strategies on how to become energized, excited, and exuberant about life
Do not be afraid

The first thing to do to become energized, excited, and exuberant about life is do not be afraid! Once again, we see why getting rid of fear is the first step to living a F.I.E.R.C.E. lifestyle. So many people have tried things, failed, and then tried again. My motto is "Never Give Up!" Guess what? You cannot give up and I will not allow you to give up. There is greatness inside of you and it is time for you to shine. Do not be afraid to start your business, write your book, love again, trust someone, or invest in yourself. You are worth it!

> *"If at first you don't succeed, try, try again!"*
> • William Edward Hickson •

Love life

The second thing to do to become energized, excited, and exuberant about life is love life. It is true that life can be scary and challenging, but you have a purpose to fulfill and the world needs you. See, living a F.I.E.R.C.E. lifestyle is comprised of six strategies whereas each step is contingent upon the previous strategy. God knew exactly what He was doing when He had me develop the women's movement. So far, we have become Fearless, discovered we are Innovative, understand the

importance of being Empowered, discovered how to be Resilient during life's tests, and exert a Confident attitude about our self and life. Now, we are motivated and energized to live life in an Exuberant way. After all of that, you cannot help but to be on fire, empowered, purpose driven, and love life.

> *"We love life, not because we are used to living but because we are used to loving."*
>
> • Friedrich Nietzsche •

Forgive yourself

The third thing to do to become energized, excited, and exuberant about life is forgive yourself. Things in life may not have turned out quite how you planned. Guess what? That is okay.

> *"To every thing there is a season, and a time to every purpose under the heaven"*
>
> • Ecclesiastes 3:1, King James Version •

When I was little, we often dreamed of the American dream of having a house with a white picket fence, a dog, husband, and two kids. That is not reality. Dream big. Do not limit yourself to the confinement of life within a box or set perimeters. Things might not have gone how you planned, but there is still time to dream again and start over. The time has come to execute your vision and bring it to fruition. It is never too late to start again. I

am 47 years old and writing my first book, earning my doctoral degree, and finally living life like it is golden. Forgive yourself for the mistakes of your past and go get your life back.

> *"When you forgive, you in no way change the past – but you sure change the future."*
>
> • **Bernard Meltzer** •

The fourth thing to do to become energized, excited, and exuberant about life is get a jumpstart. When a car will not start, sometimes the battery needs a jump. After temporarily connecting the battery to another external power source, the battery is revived and the car starts. You need a jumpstart. Hook up with some friends that you trust (or your mentor/coach) and allow them to impart into you and pray for you. True friends want to see you succeed and give you the push you need to be successful. True friends are able and willing to give you the jumpstart you need to pursue your dreams and passion. Your mentor/coach wants the best for you and is in your life to serve as a midwife to push you into your destiny.

If you do not have a coach, visit my website www.FierceWomenEmp.com to learn more about my coaching program.

While writing this book, I was stuck and overwhelmed. One day I sent a text to several people and asked them to help me with

a project by providing five words they would use to describe me. I was overwhelmed with their responses. Their words of affirmation gave me the jumpstart I needed at that moment to press forward. God puts people in our lives to encourage and motivate us. Check your external power source and stay connected to people who speak life into you.

> *"Do me a favor – right now, today, start a list of all your crazy obsessions, the things that get your heart pumping, that wake you up in the middle of the night. Put it above your desk and use it to guide you, to jumpstart your [life] each and every day."*
> • Jennifer McMahon •

Value life and yourself

The final thing to do to become energized, excited, and exuberant about life is value life and yourself. Greet each morning with a smile. Thank your Creator for awakening you. Embrace each new day because it is full of new mercies and great opportunities to walk in your purpose. Be great! Allow yourself to be happy. Sing. Dance. Love again. Laugh hard. Stop tripping and stressing over everything. Live! Yes, what made me love me was learning to smile, trust, love, and redeveloping my love for life that was not based on a person, but my own happiness.

> *"And one day she discovered that she was fierce, and strong, and full of fire, and that not even she could hold herself back because her passion burned brighter than her fears."*
>
> • **Mark Anthony** •

Coming Back as the Whole Fire

On several occasions with different projects, I had drive and determination to make a change and do things that changed the status quo of so much with life. I was on fire, my spark was lit, and I was ready to go all in. According to Urban Dictionary, on fire is defined as "a term used when someone is doing great and they are unable to be stopped." Life is about connections and having the right people connected to you. I guess my strong personality, no nonsense attitude, focus, confidence, and Spirit of excellence was too much for people because they came with fire extinguishers and put out my fire.

When I was in my cocoon stage, I did not want to do anything anymore. I had retreated and given in, but I never gave up. There is a huge difference between giving in and giving up. Remember the quote at the beginning of this chapter?

> *"It's ok if you fall down and lose your spark. Just make sure that when you get back up, you rise as the whole damn fire."*
>
> • **Colette Werden** •

I lost my spark, but I never lost hope. I fell, but I knew I needed to get back up. I felt like I had let God down and that hurt me more than anything. I knew my daughter was concerned about me so I smiled to hide my pain.

Since taking on a F.I.E.R.C.E. lifestyle whereas my mentality changed, my spark has been relit, and I have risen as an intense fire and I am stronger than before.

No longer will I operate in fear of people not understanding my calling (Fearless).

What has been placed in me has sparked a new level of creativity and I am uber excited about this movement (Innovative).

When life's attacks hit, I understand the importance of speaking to the situation as well as daily positioning myself before the Father in prayer (Empowered).

Things will occur in life because there is a time and season for everything (Ecclesiastes 3), but I will not allow negative occurrences make me retreat but instead make sure my come back game is strong (Resilient).

Looking at the woman in the mirror helps me learn to love her and hold my head up (Confident).

Developing a love for life and myself helped release positive energy and helped renew my perspective of life (Exuberant).

All of this helped me pin my motivational slogan – "No one will stop me … not even me." The time has come to walk away from what I have known life to be and begin to embrace the newness surrounding me. #FIERCE

Rules for Being Exuberant

- Do not live life inside of a box. No more jack in the box mentality.
- Listen to sound reason. Surround yourself with positive people who will help you grow.
- Laugh often.
- Do not allow anyone or anything the opportunity to steal your joy.
- Life is a gift. Love life.
- Live life to the fullest.
- Journal your thoughts, experiences, and feelings on a daily basis. Analyze your feelings.
- Speak positively. Is the glass half empty or half full? Change your perspective.
- Invest in yourself. Get a facial, massage, manicure, pedicure, a new outfit, or a new hair style. Do something for you.
- Work out. Join a fitness program or gym. Exercise is good for you.

- Change your diet. Make eating healthier a part of your daily regimen.
- Stay on top of your physical health. Make routine health and dental visits.
- Spend time with family and friends.
- Write down your plans and goals. (Write the vision and make it plain.)
- Set S.M.A.R.T. goals. S.M.A.R.T. is an acronym for Specific Measurable Attainable Realistic Timely.
- Create a vision board. Having things in your face reminds you of your goals.
- Hold yourself accountable.
- Do not be afraid to love again.
- Pray without ceasing.
- Be thankful and grateful.
- Stay humble.
- Love yourself and others.
- Be better; not bitter.
- Treat people how you want them to treat you.
- Try something new that will help you overcome your fear of something.
- Believe in Yourself.

- Haters are going to hate no matter what you do. Let your haters motivate you to reach your goals.
- Recite your daily affirmations.
- Forgive yourself and those who have wronged you.
- Hug yourself daily.
- Have a sense of humor.
- Do you. Free your mind.
- Soar. Research the eagle.
- Break free from old mentalities. Research the transformation process of the butterfly.
- Know your worth.
- Never Give Up!
- Greet each day with a smile.
- Wake, Pray, and Slay daily.
- Live life victoriously.
- Do not be afraid to shine.
- Shine bright like a diamond.
- Spend quality time with yourself.
- Do not be afraid to be alone.
- Spend time alone and getting to know you.
- Accept rebuke and correction that will make you a better person.

- Never settle for less.
- Discuss your feelings with someone you trust.
- Trust God through the process of healing, restoration, and wholeness He will take you through.
- Understand you deserve to be happy.
- Allow yourself to go through each stage of the healing and restoration process so you do not become stuck.
- Do not revert or retreat. Stand firm in your happiness and freedom.
- Smile.
- Do not be afraid. It will be okay.
- Subscribe to positive newsletters or women's groups on social media. Distract yourself from the negativity and drama and find great tools that will impart into you and build you up.
- Find a great mentor/coach.
- Forgive those who have wronged you. Forgiveness does not make what occurred correct, it allows you to be free. ("Blessed are ye, when men shall revile you, and persecute you, and shall say all manner of evil against you falsely, for my sake" Matthew 5:11, King James Version.)

- Get an accountability partner.
- Some days you might feel like a failure. You are not a failure! There is greatness inside of you.
- Get out of your own way.
- Remain teachable.
- Make peace with your past.
- Determine what the missing link is that makes you feel incomplete, and once you know what it is; find positive solutions to help you move forward.

"For whatsoever is born of God overcometh the world and this is the victory that overcometh the world, even our faith"

• 1 John 5:4, King James Version •

Daily affirmations

Daily affirmations are a great way to renew your mind from thinkinh negatively. Recite this new list for the next three days.

I am beautiful.
I am successful.
I am smart.
I am a lender and not a borrower.
I am above and not beneath.
I am wealthy.
I am on the road to discovering my identity and love for self.

I love me.
I am not the lies that have been spoken over me.
I will not believe the lies others have said to me.
I will no longer walk in fear.
I am not a failure.
I am creative.
I am renewing my mind.
I am victorious.
I am able to recover from difficult situations.
I walk in confidence.
I know who I am.
I am refined.
I am valuable.
I know my worth.
I am energetic.
I am excited about my future.
I am brilliant.
I, (your name), am a success story – not a tragedy.
I am Fearless.
I am Innovative.
I am Empowered.
I am Resilient.
I am Confident.
I am Exuberant.
I am F.I.E.R.C.E.!

Reflection

How did you feel stating the affirmations? Was it hard looking at yourself in the mirror? Were you being truthful and transparent? Journal and reflect on the experience here...

_____
_____
_____
_____
_____
_____
_____
_____
_____
_____
_____
_____
_____

LIFE APPLICATION:

What are you going to do to break through your glass ceiling to become exuberant?

In this section, journal what you will do to break through and become exuberant and develop a love for life?

It is time to put what we have discussed and what you journaled into action. This will become your action plan as you prepare and apply what you have learned to receive your break through.

_____

_____

_____

_____

_____

_____

_____

_____

_____

_____

Exuberant Prayer

Father, You said if we decree a thing it shall be established. I decree that I am being renewed in my strength. I decree and declare that I am soaring on wings like eagles. I declare that I am running the race not growing weary, and You have allowed me to walk and not faint. I declare that I shall live and not die and declare the works of the Lord. I declare that my purpose shall live and not be aborted. I declare victory over anything that is causing me to be stagnant. Father, renew my whole being and give me a new passion for all that You have set before me. Renew my spirit, Lord, make me ready for the new. Hallelujah! The joy of the Lord rests on me. The joy of the Lord is my strength. I know, Lord, that whom the Son sets free is free indeed. So, I walk in freedom in every area of my life. Amen

1 Corinthians 13

¹ Though I speak with the tongues of men and of angels, and have not charity, I am become as sounding brass, or a tinkling cymbal.

² And though I have the gift of prophecy, and understand all mysteries, and all knowledge; and though I have all faith, so that I could remove mountains, and have not charity, I am nothing.

³ And though I bestow all my goods to feed the poor, and though I give my body to be burned, and have not charity, it profiteth me nothing.

⁴ Charity suffereth long, and is kind; charity envieth not; charity vaunteth not itself, is not puffed up,

⁵ Doth not behave itself unseemly, seeketh not her own, is not easily provoked, thinketh no evil;

⁶ Rejoiceth not in iniquity, but rejoiceth in the truth;

⁷ Beareth all things, believeth all things, hopeth all things, endureth all things.

⁸ Charity never faileth: but whether there be prophecies, they shall fail; whether there be tongues, they shall cease; whether there be knowledge, it shall vanish away.

⁹ For we know in part, and we prophesy in part.

¹⁰ But when that which is perfect is come, then that which is in part shall be done away.

¹¹ When I was a child, I spake as a child, I understood as a child, I thought as a child: but when I became a man, I put away childish things.

¹² For now we see through a glass, darkly; but then face to face: now I know in part; but then shall I know even as also I am known.

¹³ And now abideth faith, hope, charity, these three; but the greatest of these is charity.

WHAT MADE ME LOVE ME: ANALYZING THE PROCESS

"Love yourself. It is important to stay positive because beauty comes from the inside out."

• Jean Proske •

What is love?

According to Google Dictionary, love is defined as "an intense feeling of deep affection."

"And now these three remain: faith, hope, and love. But the greatest of these is love"

• 1 Corinthians 13:13, New International Version •

Love shows concern for others and has the ability to transform the hardest hearts. Martin Luther King Jr. once said, "Love is the only force capable of transforming an enemy into a friend." This is so true because I was once an enemy to myself, but once I became my friend, my life changed. Due to the lack of familial love, I did not think anyone liked or loved me, and it was hard for me to receive true concern or love from other people. Even though it was hard for me to receive love, oftentimes, it was my love for people and my kind heart that had me in certain situations.

Childhood Experience

I was hung me from the fourth floor window for no apparent reason. I was tossed like a ball and dropped on my head. Although it seemed strange, my family had a weird way of showing love. I guess I wanted what was seen on television or how I saw other families interact with each other. At an older age, I began to analyze things and discovered the source of the discord that separated us.

Unconsciously, I began to build a wall around me so no one could get too close to me. My own family did not like me so I did not care if anyone else liked me. My worldview was to shield myself from experiencing further hurt, pain, rejection, and disappointment. Eventually, my attitude toward life slowly became cold and opened the door for other areas of abandonment, neglect, and even abuse. Unknowingly, eventually, my life transformed and I received healing from my past when I went through my own method of transformational learning of recognizing, analyzing, and making changes to the way I was behaving.

Identifying the Experience

I did not notice or identify my family's behavior when I was young. As a teenager, I began to identify their dislike and began to defend myself. My pain had turned into rage and resentment, and I became more conscious of how people treated me. In 8th

grade someone wrote in my Autograph book, "You are nice, but sometimes you are too nice and people take advantage of you." This opened my eyes and I began to analyze the people who were around me as well as my surroundings in a broader aspect.

Analyzing my Feelings

Before long, I began to look for the missing piece of my identity and ventured on a quest for love. Although other family members loved me, there was a piece of me that longed for those who disliked me to love me to the point that it often tormented me. Everyone wants to be loved by their family. I always wondered what I did to them to make them hate and resent me.

#MeToo

From what I recall, nothing happened, but all of a sudden a repressed memory of an instance when a family friend almost molested me when I was around 12 years old began to flood my mind. I was asleep on the couch and I felt a hand going up my shorts. I moved and opened my eyes. The man was walking back to the other couch and sat down acting like he was watching television. I was so afraid that I never said anything and eventually got up and went into the other room. When I was in my early twenties, this occurrence was haunting me like it had just occurred. It was replaying over and over in my head. During this time, I was experiencing all of the feelings of a victim –

guilt, shame, and fear. I never told anyone until I was older. Unfortunately, his face is still etched in my mind.

One day at school concert, in a room full of people, the guy sitting next to me (whom I did not know) began rubbing my knee repetitively for several minutes. I was so scared that I did not say anything. Eventually, he stopped before he left.

While talking on a payphone one day, a guy sitting in a car reached out of the car and felt on my butt. I turned in shock and disbelief. His friend apologized for him. The guy said, "I'm sorry. I just wanted to see if it was real."

Just like no one knows what an offender is thinking when he/she violates someone. No one can say how a person should react. Oftentimes, the victim is in shock and the mind represses the memory to protect the person. I had forgotten about the incident in the auditorium until I started writing this book. When thinking about it, I can see the darkness of the auditorium and a hand on my knee.

By the time I was an adult, I began to seek love from men and I was also looking for them to protect me. I would tell a guy what happened to me, and if he told me he loved me and would protect me, I felt safe and he had won my heart. Soon, these same men began to abuse me either sexually, financially, mentally, verbally, physically, and eventually Spiritually. Now, I had nowhere to run, no one to protect me, and I was still feeling

unloved. My mind was swimming with so many emotions that one day I attempted suicide.

Poem...
Conversation between my Inner Self and my Outer Self
When they see me, do they see what I see?
Do they see my flaws and imperfections?
Do they see my struggles and my pain?
Can they see what I see?
I still feel the after effects of having my finger pulled out of socket.
I saw the tears from years of wondering about my family's lack of love for me.
I felt the hit to the ear that left my ear ringing and throbbing.
I saw the stares and the eyes roll due to hatred, jealousy, and envy.
I felt the tearing of my soul as I wondered what the missing link was.
Since my perception has changed, I view things differently.
I see the effects of self-love and determination.
I feel an abundance of love from my Father.
Although I see scars, I know the battle has been won and I am victorious.
The day I breathed and exhaled I felt peace from my father's death.

And although some days the thought of my past is overwhelming and it hurts,
I know my life story was for me to be able to help someone else.

• Kimberly 06.27.2018© •

Questioning my Existence

Not feeling appreciated and loved led me to questioning my existence and how did I get to this point in my life. On the day I attempted suicide, I was tired of my life. My mind was rushing with emotions and I wanted it to stop. I could no longer take the pain so I started taking pills. My plan was to increase my dosage every hour. After the second hour, I called a friend and she talked me out of it.

The day I attempted suicide was also a turning point for me. What was possibly so bad that I wanted to end my life? Hurting emotionally and mentally made me devalue my life. But, all of a sudden, I wanted to live. Honestly, I didn't want to hurt my family members who loved me just because I was hurting. Although I was still hurting, I knew I would eventually overcome it. I did not know how, but I was ready for the fight to live and be free from my tormenting thoughts.

Depression

In 2015, I was in such a deep depression that I missed a milestone in my covenant friend's life when she celebrated her 45th birthday. I was so hurt, fighting my feelings, in denial, and had withdrawn from the social scene. Her birthday is the day after my father's death anniversary and her party was around that time. That year I could barely do anything and did not have the energy to look glamorous and could barely smile. To this day I still regret not being able to pull myself together to celebrate with her. During that time, I was in school to obtain my Master's degree, dealing with my father's death, and so overwhelmed that I almost had a nervous breakdown. I did not know how to tell anyone what I was experiencing because I did not want anyone to worry about me.

Please express to someone that you trust the feelings and emotions you are experiencing when you are not feeling your best.

Please check on your friends – event the strong ones.

> ***If for any reason you are feeling depleted, depressed, and not valued or considering life is not worth living, please contact the suicide hotline to speak with someone. Your life has purpose and you can make it past how you are currently feeling. Please do not give up.*

National Suicide Prevention Hotline 1-800-273-8255

Developing a New Strategy

My mind was racing with so many emotions, especially after I remembered what the family friend did to me, that I began seeing a therapist. During this time, I was able to discuss the hurt from my past and develop new strategies for overcoming the hurt and guilt that I felt. The therapy sessions really helped me by providing someone to talk to who did not judge me, but offered alternative solutions to overcome how I was feeling.

Life had not been very fair to me at times, but I began to realize my life could have been a lot worst. Although I was hurting, I could have lost my mind or been dead. I began to dig really deep and do some self-reflecting. The time I took to heal helped me realize a lot about life. It was also during that time that I developed a relationship with God. I was a new babe in Christ and loving it. Eventually, the enemy had set new traps. At one point, I thought I had finally found true love, but abuse soon followed. I began to think there was something wrong with me to keep encountering abusive relationships.

I Want to Know What Love Is

My daughter's life helped me see life with a new perspective and helped me understand my life had a purpose. It was not just me anymore. I had to find a reason to live and she was my reason. She did not ask to be born. She needed me. At a young age, I knew God had plans for her life. I needed to help her fulfill her

purpose. On many occasions, God used my daughter to speak life to me and give me prophetic words. One day my daughter told me, "I was in Heaven with God and He sent me to earth to show you love." She was around nine years old and did not know my battle of not feeling loved and my quest for receiving love. This was my wake up call.

Renewed and Rejuvenated by the Word of God

All of a sudden, my mind was renewed and rejuvenated and I gained strength I never knew I had. No longer was I going to be anyone's victim. I began to strengthen myself even more by reading and researching the Word of God. God's Word gave me strength to endure life's obstacles.

So often, we want to give in and give up, but that does not help the situation at hand. If we keep obtaining the same (negative) result from our actions, then it is time to rationalize and make changes. Now that I had a daughter to raise, I knew I needed to think differently about choices I made and make better decisions for both of us so I would not continue to be in a whirlwind of life. When my last relationship ended in 2002, I repented to God, apologized to my daughter, and focused on making a better life for my daughter and me. My life has definitely had trials and tribulations since then, but I have a more secure anchor than I did before. My anchor is now in Jesus Christ so when life does hit me hard, I know exactly Who to turn my face and prayers to.

Impacting Others' Lives for Change

In 2011, I founded a mentoring program to help young girls understand their life has purpose and to help them develop a closer relationship with God. I have found that so many youth, even adults; do not think their life has a purpose. I know that feeling because I used to feel the same way. My way of giving back and to avoid repeating vicious cycles is to help someone else. Empowering others is something I love to do, because I know how it is to feel alone and hopeless. If sharing my testimony helps keep someone from making the mistakes I made, then my reason for going through all I went through was to save that person's life and that makes me happy.

Developing a New Outlook on Life

Honestly, when I changed my way of thinking and no longer saw myself as a victim, I became empowered and no longer felt trapped and entangled in a web of lies and false hopes. When I decided I no longer wanted to be a victim, even to my own perceptions, my life changed. No longer did I want to be bound by hurt, deception, hatred, and rage. I wanted to love because there was so much love in me waiting to burst out. Now, I make wiser decisions because I realize the impact wrong decisions can make. The pain I endured over the years had a hefty price tag and almost ruined my life. Now, I help others recognize patterns in their own life through transformational learning.

In 2017, God saved me from me. He reconciled old friendships and resuscitated me by changing my perspective and reality (CPR). I had been behind a wall and encased in my self-made bubble for years, but God spoke a word to me that ignited a spark within me and gave me the strength and courage to live again. F.I.E.R.C.E. is not just a word; it is a lifestyle that helped me deal with depression, anxiety, and self-hatred.

The Answer to the Question

What made me love me? There are a few things that made me love me, but changing my perception of my life, making wiser decisions, learning to love me, leading with my mind instead of my heart, and letting go of the hurt from my past were the first stepping stones. Once my perception changed, I understood my worth. See, before, I did not value who I was and I felt defeated. Understanding my life had a purpose made me value my life. The things I encountered were for a reason and tied to my purpose in efforts to help someone else. The seal of the deal was when I learned about God's love for me. When I understood God's love for me, I began to see myself how He saw me – as His Masterpiece.

> *"For we are God's masterpiece. He has created us anew in Christ Jesus, so we can do the good things he planned for us long ago"*
> • Ephesians 2:10, New Living Translation •

I know what it is like to search for something that you feel is missing. I know what it is like to want a way out of an abusive relationship, but cannot find a way of escape. I understand the sting of rejection and abandonment. I know what it feels like to lose a parent and wonder will the pain ever go away. I know what it is like to want to end your life due to all of the pain you are experiencing.

Just like I eventually healed from rejection and the missing components of my life, you can rise above your situation and heal from your pain as well. What made me love me? It was when I took a stand to no longer be a victim and realized I wanted more from life than what had been dealt to me. What made me love me? It was when I decided the lifestyle I was living was not the one destined for me. What made me love me? The day I became F.I.E.R.C.E.!

[35] Who shall separate us from the love of Christ? shall tribulation, or distress, or persecution, or famine, or nakedness, or peril, or sword?
[36] As it is written, For thy sake we are killed all the day long; we are accounted as sheep for the slaughter.
[37] Nay, in all these things we are more than conquerors through him that loved us.
[38] For I am persuaded, that neither death, nor life, nor angels, nor principalities, nor powers, nor things present, nor things to come,

³⁹ Nor height, nor depth, nor any other creature, shall be able to separate us from the love of God, which is in Christ Jesus our Lord

• **Romans 8:35-39, King James Version** •

My Reflection
The Effects of Abuse

When a woman experiences abusive relationships, it tears a piece of her identity and self-confidence from her. She often wonders where she went wrong, what's wrong with her, or what she did to deserve this treatment. These feelings usually lead to depression, emptiness, loneliness, incompleteness, and suicidal thoughts. Overcoming the sting from abuse takes time, patience, love, acceptance, forgiveness, and healing.

For me, it took forgiving myself as well as those who had abused me. It took being okay with never hearing "I'm sorry" and understanding there was not anything wrong with me that caused them to behave the way that they did. It took understanding my life had purpose even when others did not value my life. And it took me allowing God to heal me from the pain, shame, hurt, and anguish that I felt. Restoration was what I needed more than anything, but God took it a step further and He made me whole, complete, and lacking nothing (James 1:4; Matthew 9:22).

There was a point in my life when I never wanted anything much from life because I was hurting so badly and I felt as though I did not deserve much of anything from life. This was my mentality for years, but no one knew it. I was suffering in silence. One day God renewed my mind and reassured me I was not who others were making me out to be. God restored my confidence, love for self, and joy. During this process, I was able to learn more about love, relationships, life, and myself. As God had me gleaning, He saturated me with love, patience, and understanding to a point that I was able to minister to women in different ways to restore them and their relationships.

A Change is Gon' Come

In my adult years, I began to really analyze my life. I realized the love my family and I had for each was different and could not be compared to other's perception of familial love. What I often considered as dysfunctional was due to years of masked hurt, rejection, and abandonment that we were dealing with. It is said that hurt people hurt people and that had been the cycle within my family. Now, I am able to say it is not that certain family members did not love me, but instead did not know how to love others or themselves.

In 2017, when God told me reconciliation would occur in my life, I saw old friendships mended, and I was so happy. I also experienced the dissolution of two friendships that tore

at me to the core, but I did not allow it to break me. Writing this book exposed empty areas, areas that needed healing and areas that needed forgiveness. Little did I know 2018 would award me the opportunity to learn so much about myself, launching the women's movement, writing my first book, locating family members I had been searching for the last eight years, discovering the missing link in my life, a broken friendship reconciled, and discovering true love.

Life can be challenging at times whereas you might not know the exact way to implement change or bring restoration/reconciliation. Stay prayerful and examine how you contributed to the situation. Remember – the best way to be honest with others is to be honest with yourself.

New Attitude for Life

During my 15 years of not dating, I learned who I was and took the time to heal from the abusive relationships I had been in. I learned what made me tick, my likes and dislikes, spent time getting to know me, and learned my worth. I learned so much about myself and checked myself when I was exerting a stank attitude. I grew so much and became stronger mentally, Spiritually, and emotionally. My tolerance level for nonsense was very low and still is to this day which helped me see things for its face value. I do not have time for the games I played in high school. My focus is on continually making myself better so I can

be an example for my daughter and those I mentor. Life is short and we make what we choose to make of it. No one controls our destiny, but us.

Over the years, I have learned what I will and will not accept. I remember when people would say anything to me and I would retreat and buckle. Now, I am able to stand firm on the Word of God and confident in who He has called and positioned me to be. Situations in life used to hurt me so much that I would cry and hate myself even more. My past of encountering abusive relationships made me devalue my worth. I look back at those times and wonder who that person was. But guess what? My past is just that – in the past. I cannot change the past, but I can set the course for my future.

Changing the Status Quo

Now, I use what I have been through to help other people. Yes, I have been hit, chased, threatened, smacked, jumped on, cursed out, belittled, dropped on my head, hung from a fourth floor window, mocked, spit on, and cheated on. I have jumped from moving cars and cursed people out who did me wrong. At one point, all of the negativity around me made me feel less than, but God had a different plan. God picked me up, dusted me off, changed my perspective, renewed my mind, and positioned me for purpose. Just when the odds seemed to be stacked against me, God changed the status quo of my life.

This book is purpose driven. I found peace along my journey of discovering and establishing self-empowerment and self-love and I hope the same for everyone who reads this book. What made me love me? Understanding my life had purpose, becoming F.I.E.R.C.E., loving myself, and understanding God's love for me are what made me love me. Now, it is time for you to learn to love you. What will make you love you?

Life Lesson - Transparency

The most important thing life has taught me is the importance of transparency and truth. When I was 'real' about things, it seems people could not handle the truth. It made me wonder why people prefer to live in fabricated scenarios that they feel are the truth. The truth is precious, pure, and so necessary. I do not want to live within the constraints of a lie in any aspect of my life. Lies lead to mistrust. Transparency reveals so much. You never know who needs your testimony. Being real about your ups and downs can help so many people. I share my testimony so others will not be in the bondage I was once in.

Rules for Loving Yourself when No One Else Does

- You owe it to yourself to love you
- Know your worth
- Speak life to your situation
- Love you no matter what

What is your Life Built on?

> To every thing there is a season, and a time to every purpose under the heaven:
>
> ² A time to be born, and a time to die; a time to plant, and a time to pluck up that which is planted;
>
> ³ A time to kill, and a time to heal; a time to break down, and a time to build up;
>
> ⁴ A time to weep, and a time to laugh; a time to mourn, and a time to dance;
>
> ⁵ A time to cast away stones, and a time to gather stones together; a time to embrace, and a time to refrain from embracing;
>
> ⁶ A time to get, and a time to lose; a time to keep, and a time to cast away;
>
> ⁷ A time to rend, and a time to sew; a time to keep silence, and a time to speak;
>
> ⁸ A time to love, and a time to hate; a time of war, and a time of peace
>
> • Ecclesiastes 3:1-8, King James Version •

Life's challenges can either build up or tear things down. The foundation on which something is built is very important. If the foundation is strong, it can withstand different seasons. There might be some damage to the structure, but the foundation, especially if it is solid, it essential. If the foundation is weak, it will not withstand the storms of life (this pertains to a building as well as our personal life).

"And I say also unto thee, That thou art Peter, and upon this rock I will build my church; and the gates of hell shall not prevail against it"
• Matthews 16:18, King James Version •

Do you recall the fable, *The Three Little Pigs?* Each pig built their house and the amount of time spent to build the house was evident. The first house was built with hay, the second house was built with twigs, and the third house was built with bricks. The first two pigs laughed at the third pig because he worked hard and never had time to play. Although the third pig's house took longer to build, he knew he was building a strong foundation for what was to come.

> [47] Whosoever cometh to me, and heareth my sayings, and doeth them, I will shew you to whom he is like:
> [48] He is like a man which built an house, and digged deep, and laid the foundation on a rock: and when the flood arose, the stream beat vehemently upon that house, and could not shake it: for it was founded upon a rock.
> [49] But he that heareth, and doeth not, is like a man that without a foundation built an house upon the earth; against which the stream did beat vehemently, and immediately it fell; and the ruin of that house was great.
> • Luke 6:47-49, King James Version •

My question to you is - what kind of foundation are you building? Is everything you do based off of right now or are you planning for your future? Are you utilizing the gifts God

gave you or are you continuously too busy enjoying life in the moment?

Remember we talked about the Proverbs 31 Woman? A F.I.E.R.C.E. woman is likened to the Proverbs 31 Woman whereas she is resourceful, exercises great time management skills, simultaneously plans and prepares for her now and her future, takes care of her family and others, and builds and structures her life based on a strong foundation so it can withstand life's challenges.

Journal how you will plan and prepare your future so it is built on a strong foundation…

_____
_____
_____
_____
_____
_____
_____
_____
_____
_____
_____
_____
_____
_____
_____
_____
_____
_____

Moving Forward

While writing this book, I had to fight. I had to fight for my finances, my peace, and my health. I had to come out of my comfort zone and network. As I opened my mouth, God filled it. As I submitted my will to His will, God opened new doors of opportunity. My "yes" was tested, but my "yes" was planted on good ground and was reaping a harvest. As I write the final sections and make edits, I reflect on the good, the bad, and the ugly of my life, and I rejoice in each part of my life because I know it is going to get better. God is faithful. His promises are yea and amen. I trust Him. Do you trust Him? Do you trust Him enough to submit your will for His?

During the final stages of finishing the final version of this book, so many emotions came upon me. So many thoughts ran through my mind. Remember on certain cartoon episodes there would be an angel on one shoulder and the devil on the other shoulder of the character? LOL I experienced many days like that. The enemy was trying to discourage me and I felt like I was having a Job experience whereas I was being tested by God. One thing carried me through those times – my faith. I wanted to give up, but my motto is #NeverGiveUp. There was so much invested and too much at stake. The more the enemy tried to discourage me, the more I chiseled out God's plan for this book and the women's movement. At one point I stopped editing the final version, but I was always writing something on a sticky note

or mapping out the agenda for the Launch, but I never stopped doing something to bring this vision to fruition.

You see, I could not look at the small picture which was the different attacks I was going through. I had to look at the big picture – people being set free and walking in their purpose. Too many lives were at stake if I did not complete this book and launch the women's movement.

Pressing past what I was experiencing was just a test of living a F.I.E.R.C.E. lifestyle.

- A. Could I be Fearless while walking in my purpose?
- B. Could I be Innovative by creating a movement that would transform lives?
- C. Could I Empower myself in the midst of a stormy season?
- D. Could I be Resilient and bounce back from the fiery darts being thrown at me?
- E. Could I be Confident in who God called me to be?
- F. Could I be Exuberant about life while I was going through a stormy season?

The answer is yes (G. All of the above), and I owe it to God and having a renewed mind.

> *"And he shall be like a tree planted by the rivers of water, that bringeth forth his fruit in his season; his leaf also shall not wither; and whatsoever he doeth shall prosper."*
>
> • Psalm 1:3, King James Version •

Remember I told you I could not guarantee that you would smile every day or that there would not be tests? My main goal is to help change your perspective and approach to obstacles you will encounter.

Writing my life story has not been easy, but God said, "It was necessary." Lord, I trust You. Thank You for getting me to the place of peace, self-empowerment, self-love, and resiliency. The road has been bumpy and emotional, but I understand it was necessary. Thank You for never leaving me nor forsaking me Thank You for choosing me and using me. Thank You for being the Source who made me love me. Yes, what made me love me was learning until I learned God's unconditional love for me, I could never love myself.

My Personal Declaration and Breakthrough

What made me love me - The Poem

> What made me love me?
> Was it fashion, was it gold
> Was it platinum, was it a man's hold
> Was it fortune, was it wealth
> Was it diamonds, was it good health
> Could it be bought, who had it to sell
> Could it be marriage, was it the sound of wedding bells
> Was it my friends, was it a man
> Was it my family, was it an admiring fan

What made me love me?
It didn't come from a box
It wasn't bought in a store
It wasn't anything materialistic or anything costly
It didn't come from a human being

What made me love me?
It was the day I took a stand
I listened closely to God's Voice
His Voice was soothing and calm
He gave me confidence and helped me make the right choice
My tears stopped flowing
I had direction and peace
Now, the time has come to put His plan into action
Before my determination begins to cease

What made me love me?
It was the day I stopped hating me
It was the day I stared myself in the face, affirmed me, cried, and eventually smiled
It was the day I saw me how God sees me
It was the day I began loving me

No person could put into words the way I felt that day. After all I had been going through, God confirmed that He would pave the way.
Sure, we've heard others tell of what His Word (the Bible)

tells us to do.

But when He speaks to you, you can feel His love come shining through.

Be still and know that He is God and He will carry you through.

When He speaks, listen for there is so much work to do.

• Kimberly, 07/28/00© •

Daily affirmations

I feel great when I speak positively. Here is a new list of affirmations to recite for the next threee days.

I am beautiful.
I am successful.
I am smart.
I am a lender and not a borrower.
I am above and not beneath.
I am wealthy.
I am on the road to discovering my identity and love for self.
I am not the lies that have been spoken over me.
I will not believe the lies others have said to me.
I will no longer walk in fear.
I am not a failure.
I am creative.
I am renewing my mind.
I am victorious.

I am able to recover from difficult situations.
I walk in confidence.
I know who I am.
I am refined.
I am valuable.
I know my worth.
I am energetic.
I am excited about my future.
I am brilliant.
I no longer see myself as my enemy.
I am loved.
God loves me.
I will align my will to God's will and plan for my life.
I, (your name), am a success story – not a tragedy.
I am Fearless.
I am Innovative.
I am Empowered.
I am Resilient.
I am Confident.
I am Exuberant.
I am F.I.E.R.C.E.!
I LOVE ME!

Reflection

How did you feel stating the affirmations? Was it hard looking at yourself in the mirror? Were you being truthful and transparent? Journal and reflect on the experience here…

_____
_____
_____
_____
_____
_____
_____
_____
_____
_____
_____
_____
_____
_____

LIFE APPLICATION:
What are you going to do to break through your glass ceiling to love yourself?

In this section, journal what you will do to exert self-love.

_____

_____

_____

_____

_____

_____

_____

_____

_____

_____

_____

_____

_____

_____

_____

Love Declaration

I love you, Lord, and I bless Your Holy name. I walk in Your love today, Father, because You first loved me. I decree and declare that the same love that God has for me flows through my veins. I declare that I have no grief, but only love. I declare that my heart is filled with love and hurt and pain are not rooted here. I declare that my mind is filled with thoughts of love and all negative thoughts are removed. I declare now that I love the way God has created me because I am created in His image. I decree and declare that my mouth will speak of the goodness of God in my life because His Love surrounds me. I declare that I walk in righteousness. I declare that I have been set free so that I can walk in freedom. I decree and declare that I am the head and not the tail. I declare that I no longer walk in darkness. I declare that I have an abundance of life. I decree and declare that I have forgiven myself. I declare that I abide in Christ and He abides in me. I declare that I am walking in the pathway set before me. I decree and declare that I will continually love myself as God first loved me! The love of God surrounds me daily. Amen

"I knew you before I formed you in your mother's womb!"

TIME FOR RESTORATION AND RENEWAL

The Prophecy that changed my life

It has been really hard to write this book. In 2003, while on a fast, God revealed something very important to me.

He said, "I am going to peel you like a banana. There are layers of pain that need to be removed to get to the core of who you really are. You are anointed and gifted and I am going to bring that out of you. You are holding on to the pain and the anguish and you are afraid of moving ahead. I said in My Word, 'that I would never leave you nor forsake you' and I mean that. I know all that you have been through, and it was a process to get you to where I am taking you. Kim, you need to let go. You need to let go of it all. You are afraid of failure and afraid of falling. I have you. Trust Me and believe in Me! I have great plans for you My child. PROCESS! You are being processed. First, we are going to shed the pounds that have brought you to not like who you see in the mirror. Then, we are going to deal with the pain that has left you feeling ashamed. Don't worry about the friends you have lost, I have removed them from your life for a reason. Stop being like the children of Israel, and always looking back. Stop dwelling on the past. Stop feeling like you are nothing and nobody. I Am the Great I AM and I created you in My Own image, in My likeness. Once I have removed the pain you've endured; I will work on your heart. In your heart, there is so much fear, hurt, pain, mistrust, anguish, and confusion. You know who you and where I want to take you, but the pain of the past keeps holding you back. You take two steps closer to Me, and then you freeze. I am going to change all of that. As a child you learned how to walk by taking it one step at a time. I am going to teach you how to walk all over again. Your steps will be ordered by Me. You will know when you hear My voice, and you will move accordingly. Now once all of that is done, I will be at the core of who you are and I will rise up a new creation. You have been talking about this birthing in your belly that you have been feeling. That is the fire of the Holy Ghost burning inside of you ready to get out. Once I have finished processing you, you will be a new creation. Behold I am doing a new thing... I am doing a new thing in you. The gifts you have now will flourish into full being. You will prophesy. You will pray in your prayer language. Your gift of discernment will be enhanced. People will not recognize you for they will see a difference. You will walk in confidence of My Word. You will teach with authority, truth, love, and conviction. I will tell you what I want My people to hear. The ministry that I have appointed to you will draw so many unto me; for that is why I called it Spirit Led to be Human Fed. My child, I have great plans to prosper you and give you an expected end. You have to believe in Me. Without faith it is impossible to please Me. You have the faith, but you doubt that

My plans of prosperity will grow upon you and within you. I love you, My child. Yes, people have talked about you, they have deceived you, they have hurt you; but you need to let Me worry about that and stop sweating the small stuff. You told Me you were ready. Ready to be used by Me. I heard that prayer. I have so much to tell you. Are you ready to receive your harvest? Kim, it is harvest time. Are you ready to reap what you have sown?"

March 24, 2003

****Sometimes people can relate to the Word of the Lord that has been spoken to someone else, which is the reason I shared this.*

The Prophecy that will Change Your Life

Just as God spoke to me about the process he was going to take me through almost 15 years ago, He is saying to you…

"The time has come for you to believe in Me. The time has come for you to trust Me. There is so much that I have in store for you. I am going to awaken you and open your eyes to see not only in the natural, but Spiritually as well. I am doing a new thing in, through, and around you. I am going to change so much about you, including your taste buds. I am going to break off the desires of your flesh and grant you the desires of your heart. This process will be a renewing of your mind to bring about total healing, restoration and wholeness in every area of your life. Do you trust Me? Do you believe Me? Do you believe

that I can do exceeding abundantly above all you could ever ask or think? From this process, not only will you be restored, but you will be fierce in a manner that you are more than a conqueror and you will realize you are an overcomer. I love you and I want the best for you. The time has come for you to change the status quo of your life and see things as I see them. You have tunnel vision. I am going to broaden your spectrum. Are you ready?

November 25, 2017

CALL TO SALVATION

Maybe you are reading this book and have never known of the God that is spoken of in this book. Or maybe you knew Him, but for some reason or another, you are not in a right relationship with Him right now. Maybe you have experienced church hurt and vowed to never set foot in a church building again. I do not want you to miss out on getting to know God or restoring your relationship with Him. Oftentimes, we are told God does not hear a sinner's prayer. I was told that and believed it for years. Until one day God said to me, "If I did not listen to a sinner's prayer, how would I hear you when you prayed to me to come out of the sin or situation you are in?" These words gave me the strength to overcome and leave the sin I was in because before my mentality was – I guess I will stay stuck in this life since God does not hear my prayers. I am so glad I learned to hear the voice of the Lord as well as the truth of His Word.

Say this prayer…

Lord, thank You for loving me when I did not love myself. Lord, thank you for keeping me from hurt, harm, and danger. Lord, thank you for thinking of me and choosing me even though I have failed You numerous times. I have learned Your love is unfailing and I thank You for never giving up on me. You never cease to amaze me. Lord, I know I have done wrong and sinned in Your sight and I am sorry for all that I have done that is not

pleasing unto You. Lord, I need Your help and guidance. In the past, I trusted and believed the wrong things, but I thank You for Your Word which says, "trust in the Lord with all thine heart and lean not to thine own understanding. In all thy ways acknowledge Him and He will direct thy path." Lord, I trust You. Lord, I know the only way my life will change is with You in it navigating me along the right path. Lord, I believe in You and Your Word. I acknowledge Your Son who died on Calvary's cross for the remission of my sins. I confess with my mouth and believe in my heart that You raised Jesus from the grave. Lord, I love You and I cannot go on this journey of life without You. Lord, I want to establish (renew my) a relationship with You. Please forgive me of all my sins and faults. I need You, Lord. Amen

You are now in right standing with God.

The process does not stop there. Read God's Word on a daily basis and continue to walk on the right path. Old things have passed away. All things become new today.

Welcome to the Kingdom of God!

F.I.E.R.C.E.
WOMEN'S EMPOWERMENT MOVEMENT

Our Purpose

God has heard the cry of the wailing women, hurting women, discouraged women, and broken women. As women, we set the tone for so much within our families, businesses, and careers. When women are depleted, the balance and rhythm of our lives are out of sync. For this reason, the F.I.E.R.C.E. Women's Empowerment Movement was established.

Our Mission

F.I.E.R.C.E. Women's Empowerment Movement has been commissioned to empower women across the nations. Our past experiences, daily interactions, and life in general strip us of our identities, faith, hope, aspirations, and dreams. Without a support system, these trials can lead to depression, loss of motivation, confusion, and discouragement. F.I.E.R.C.E. Women's Empowerment Movement was created as an avenue to empower women and provide a support system of resources for life's daily encounters that might have women questioning life. This movement is dear to our heart and it is our prayer that as you view the website, interact on the blog, and wear your F.I.E.R.C.E. apparel that you will be inspired and empowered to

overcome life's tests and trials. This movement is structured to serve as a catalyst for empowerment, support, and inspiration, and to let you know that you are not alone as you face different life encounters. F.I.E.R.C.E. Women's Empowerment Movement strives to empower women to be bold, ferocious, empowered, inspired, purpose-driven, and confident. Won't you join us in this movement to transform and empower the lives of women around the world?

F.I.E.R.C.E. Women's Empowerment Movement is a renewing of the mind to change the negative mindset into a positive mindset (Romans 12:1-3). Instead of being depleted, depressed, broken, weak, walking in low self-esteem, and not understanding our purpose or worth we strive to be extremely fabulous, high fashion, highly creative, operating in a Spirit of Excellence, walking in extreme confidence, and strong. Our mission is to be women of provision and wisdom like the Proverbs 31 woman (Proverbs 31:10-31).

Different meanings for fierce include...

Bold • Outstanding • Cool • Awesome • Fearless
Looking fly or good
Someone who is on fire and possess a lot of swag
Different • Daring • Highly creative
Oozing with charisma
Attract the masses in an instant
Stand out from the crowd for all the right reasons

Message from Kimberly Rashawn
Founder and Executive Director

I used to be timid and shy and I had to learn the proper way of speaking up for myself because people would use my kindness for weakness. At one point, I was determined I would try my best to be better and not bitter, but hurt led to anger and anger led to rage, and I was losing control of myself. Abusive relationships and failed friendships made me feel defeated, unappreciated, and angry. After years of merely existing, I decided it was time to no longer live in isolation. One day my godfather told me I had a tiger's pounce in how I handled myself and began to explain how it was a complement as to my nature and delivery method of speaking up for myself and getting my point across. Soon thereafter, I heard "FIERCE." I looked up the meaning of the word "fierce" and the Lord began to speak. The time has come for women to network and empower each other for greater works. This movement is a spark that will ignite change within our communities, homes, workplace, and families. #FIERCE

About Brianna Darling
Marketing Director

Being a woman who has been short all of her life and standing only 5 feet tall, I have often heard the word 'feisty' to describe me. For a while, I let people use that word to

describe me because I believed it described my spunk, courage, determination, and gutsy behavior. But I no longer want to be known or described as being feisty due to the negative aspect it can hold. Instead, I want to know as being F.I.E.R.C.E. because I am not just the adjectives that I previously described; I am so much more. I am Fearless (for God has not given me a spirit of fear), Innovative (I have a creative and inventive mind), Empowered (I am self-empowered and possess the ability to empower others), Resilient (I bounce back), Confident (I am comfortable with the skin I am in), Exuberant (I am full of energy ... I am a light ready to shine and guide others).

ABOUT THE AUTHOR

"Focused, determined, and purpose driven to serve God with all of my heart and help others discover their purpose is what I strive to do daily."

Kimberly Rashawn, M.Ed., BCPC

Let your light so shine before men, that they may see your good works, and glorify your Father which is in heaven…

• **Matthew 5:16** •

Kimberly Rashawn is a social entrepreneur, board certified professional coach, minister of dance, radio personality, author, speaker, and organizational development consultant.

Since answering her calling to serve in ministry in 1998, Kimberly has hit the ground running and serves God with an adoration and passion that is contagious. She discovered her gifts of administration, teaching, working with youth, and empowering others to walk in their purpose during her time of training.

From 2000-2010, Kimberly served as the founder and director of Spirit Led 2 B Human Fed Ministry (SL2BHF), which served to inspire, encourage, and edify God's people to press on in spite of life's challenges.

In 2011, Kimberly birthed T.R.A.I.N. Our Youth Program. T.R.A.I.N. has been commissioned to Teach, Reach, Activate, Inspire and Nurture young ladies ages 14-25 to be all God has called them to be and provide them with a foundation of God's Word to build upon (Proverbs 22:6).

In August 2017, Kimberly joined Victory Through Christ Radio Network (www.wvtcradio.com) as a radio personality of her own broadcast, The Empowerment Hour. The Empowerment Hour serves as a catalyst to inspire, motivate, encourage, and empower listeners via discussion topics and inspirational music.

F.I.E.R.C.E. Women's Empowerment Movement has been established to empower women across the nation. F.I.E.R.C.E. (Fearless Innovative Empowered Resilient Confident Exuberant) strives to provide a support system for women facing challenging moments in their life, foster friendships, strengthen the family unit, and serve the community. This new movement will launch Fall 2018. #FIERCE #LiveFIERCE

The time finally arrived for Kimberly Rashawn to pen her life story of overcoming self-hatred, developing self-love, and living a F.I.E.R.C.E. lifestyle. Her self-published book, What Made Me Love Me: Six Strategies to Live F.I.E.R.C.E., will be released Fall 2018.

LET'S STAY CONNECTED...

It would be awesome to stay connected with you. Please like our social media pages to join our F.I.E.R.C.E. family and visit our website to subscribe to our email list so you can stay abreast with our on-line courses, conference calls, workshops, seminars, and tour information.

Follow us on social media...

Fierce_Women_Emp   Fierce Women Emp

Fierce Women's Empowerment Movement

I Am Kimberly Rashawn (Author page)

For booking or more information, please visit our website:
www.FierceWomenEmp.com

Complete List of Affirmations

I am beautiful.

I am successful.

I am smart.

I am a lender and not a borrower.

I am above and not beneath.

I am wealthy.

I am on the road to discovering my identity and love for self.

I am not the lies that have been spoken over me.

I will not believe the lies others have said to me.

I will no longer walk in fear.

I am not a failure.

I am creative.

I am renewing my mind.

I am victorious.

I am able to recover from difficult situations.

I walk in confidence.

I know who I am.

I am refined.

I am valuable.

I know my worth.

I am energetic.
I am excited about my future.
I am brilliant.
I no longer see myself as my enemy.
I am loved.
God loves me.
I will align my will to God's will and plan for my life.
I, (your name), am a success story – not a tragedy.
I am Fearless.
I am Innovative.
I am Empowered.
I am Resilient.
I am Confident.
I am Exuberant.
I am F.I.E.R.C.E.!
I LOVE ME!

www.ingramcontent.com/pod-product-compliance
Lightning Source LLC
Chambersburg PA
CBHW030317080526
44584CB00012B/595